"Theatre of Witness is a modern ph[...] of needs—the need to tell our story, to be listened to, to find healing for ourselves, and for everyone in our ability to empathize, to be generous, and find light in the darkest pit. The work of Theatre of Witness in Northern Ireland has been transformative of the lives of its participants, facilitators, the musicians, filmmakers, producers, and its audiences. It needs to be shared throughout the globe. The publication of Teya's writings will be a substantial contribution to the process of enlightenment in this mid-winter of Bible black long nights of recession."

—Eamonn Deane, founder, Holywell Trust,
Derry/Londonderry Northern Ireland

"Teya Sepinuck is a skilful and gifted artist who knows how to guide untrained participants to reveal incredible, but true, stories in a dramatic performance called: Theatre of Witness... This unique approach will bring readers to tears in some stories and joy in others in an amazing and beautiful book that opens the reader's heart and soul to experience stories that are willingly shared and artfully presented in a deeply spiritual context. What a great offering!"

—Rabbi David A. Cooper, author of God is a Verb

"Teya's writing brings to light the delicacy and daring involved in the process of creating Theatre of Witness performances. Equally important, it conveys the stories and wisdom of all of those participants who have, over the course of more than 20 years, contributed to the development of this restorative practice. This book will be a beacon and a guide for activists, students, teachers, directors, and performers. It offers an important template for those of us committed to arts for social change and peace and conflict studies work in academic institutions and community groups across the world."

—Sharon Friedler, Professor and Director of Dance, faculty
adviser for Off Campus Study, Swarthmore College

"Teya Sepinuck's *Theatre of Witness: Finding the Medicine in Stories of Suffering, Transformation, and Peace* is a thought-provoking, touching, and humanizing book that can play a valuable role in framing questions about the role of remorse, forgiveness, rehabilitation, and incarceration. In these uplifting stories of performers who have experienced the ripple effect of crime and imprisonment, the reader can find hope that change is possible."

—*M. Kay Harris, Associate Professor Emeritus, Department of Criminal Justice, Temple University, Philadelphia*

"The categories used by political actors and academics often subtly and unwittingly reinforce the sectarianism upon which deeply divided societies feed. The Theatre of Witness that Teya Sepinuck created and realized through performances in Northern Ireland helps both those who 'perform' their own stories, and the audiences who witness them, to transcend those categories and the concrete divisions they help to engender. In the process our common humanity is affirmed."

—*Dr. James Skelly, Director of the Baker Institute for Peace and Conflict Studies, Juniata College, Pennsylvania*

"*Theatre of Witness* is a wonderful journey into the hearts and souls of people living in grief and hardship but blessed with incredible dignity and strength in their quest for personal and collective transformation and community healing. The book is also a wonderful testimony to the tremendous power of performance in creating physical and emotional safe spaces for people to come together, share their stories, and emerge from the process as more alive and accomplished human beings. A courageous book by a caring and compassionate artist."

—*Hjalmar Jorge Joffre-Eichorn, theatre practitioner (Afghanistan Human Rights and Democracy Organization)*

"I am Hakim 'Ali, that big, black Muslim man that Teya referred to in this great work, sharing with you what the Theatre of Witness is all about. I am a man who is still in the midst of transforming himself, still attempting to be the best he can be, still embracing LOVE and recognizing COURAGE when it comes to the surface. I owe more than you can imagine to Teya and this troupe of performers that she makes reference to, this group of courageous women, mothers, and sisters, all victims of violence that ravished our city. I owe them my life, there is no doubt about this. No, not my existence, but my 'life', and the ability and opportunity to 'live the life of a normal man'. This was given to me by all who participated in *Beyond the Walls* and the other projects that Teya produced and directed. So, read and invest yourself, do not just read for amusement, this work is far too important for that. And, thank you Teya for being who you are and what you have done for so many... We will forever be grateful."

—*Hakim 'Ali, the voice of the voiceless and performer in* Beyond the Walls *and* Holding Up

"At last Teya Sepinuck has found time between projects to document and share what she has learnt from decades of inspirational work with marginalized groups. General readers will be fascinated and uplifted by her vivid accounts of innovative performance projects in Europe and America within the prison system and in the wider world. Practitioners will find special value in the way she has distilled her life's work into a number of profound principles which will immeasurably enrich their own practice."

—*David Grant, lecturer in Drama and Director of Education (School of Creative Arts), Queens University, Belfast, Northern Ireland*

"Teya Sepinuck and her casts show us that peace-building is an artful process that requires courage, patience, intuition, and trust. Sepinuck, in her profound way, treats every Theatre of Witness performance as a unique moment of grace, but the productions lovingly shared in this book demonstrate over and over that people have the will and capacity to heal one another. May we all be encouraged to kick at the darkness by speaking truth to our fears and injustices."

—Lee A. Smithey, Associate Professor of Sociology and Peace and Conflict Studies at Swarthmore College, and author of Unionists, Loyalists, and Conflict Transformation in Northern Ireland

Teya Sepinuck

Theatre
of Witness

Finding the Medicine in Stories of
Suffering, Transformation, and Peace

Jessica Kingsley *Publishers*
London and Philadelphia

Note: Some names of performers have been changed for reasons of confidentiality.

Photographs on pages 13, 18, 23, 32, 46 and 58 are reproduced by kind permission of Patented Photos.
Photograph on page 76 reproduced by kind permission of Lukasz Tura.
Photograph on page 91 is a patented photo, reproduced by kind permission of Ed Seiz.
Photograph on page 106 reproduced by kind permission of Craig Cullinane.
Photograph on pages 115 and 124 are taken from a video by Melvin Epps, reproduced by kind permission.
Photograph on page 131 is taken from a video by Rachel Libert, reproduced by kind permission.
Photograph on page 152 reproduced by kind permission of Oliver Orr.
Photograph on page 188 reproduced by kind permission of Brendan Harley.

First published in 2013
by Jessica Kingsley Publishers
73 Collier Street
London N1 9BE, UK
and
400 Market Street, Suite 400
Philadelphia, PA 19106, USA

www.jkp.com

Library of Congress Cataloging in Publication Data
Sepinuck, Teya.
  Theatre of witness : finding the medicine in stories of suffering, transformation and peace / Teya Sepinuck.
    pages cm
  ISBN 978-1-84905-382-2 (alk. paper)
  1. Suffering--Psychological aspects. 2. Pain--Psychological aspects. 3. Victims. I. Title.
  BF789.S8S47 2013
  155.9'3--dc23

                              2012032524

British Library Cataloguing in Publication Data
A CIP catalogue record for this book is available from the British Library

ISBN 978 1 84905 382 2
eISBN 978 0 85700 745 2

Dedicated lovingly to my sons,
Daniel and Adam Sepinuck Immerwahr

And to my teacher with the dancing eyes
and infinite heart,

Rabbi David Cooper

Contents

Prelude
Setting the Scene

I am crouching in the wings of the theatre watching the performance of *Children of Cambodia/Children of War*. From the side angle I see Hong Peach's graceful silhouette balance, as she perches on her right leg and her hands glide through the air in slow motion. Her fingers touch and trace invisible lines in the soft blue light. Her beauty is pure and lingers like perfume. Then with a boisterous shout, the Cambodian teen boys bound through the space, cajoling each other as they flip and jump over higher and higher ropes before collapsing into a pile of limbs on the floor, laughing, before one turns serious:

If this is so much fun, why can't I remember?

Tim's eyes fill with unshed tears. Haunting chords of music increase in volume.

The reason is because so many horrible things happened in our country—it keeps us from remembering the good things. Our country used to be a peaceful place to live in, but now because of the holocaust, our people are being killed one by one.

One of my first memories is seeing people dying on the street
Bullets everywhere
Piles of bones on the street…

They would line up people one by one in a straight line
With one bullet they could get many

My mom, she was holding my hand
My feet were burning
I had no clothes on…
My country is a red river with bullets and blood.

And from there, the memories pour out. Even though I've heard these stories countless times, transcribed and scripted the text, and directed the performers for hours on end, I'm riveted to my spot and almost forget to breathe. The moment is so embedded with tragedy, authenticity, and beauty, the stories are nearly unbearable, yet here are these young people, strong, resilient, and alive. They survived war, starvation, refugee camps, and the journey to this place. They want to bring us back with them. To have us bear witness. The show ends with these words, spoken and in song:

> Our eyes cry the tears. Our blood screams for our people killed. Our skin calls us back.
> We want to tell you, so we won't forget.
> We want to show you, so you'll remember.
> We will involve you so you'll understand.
> We will survive. We will survive.

And with that, the audience is on its feet. My face is wet with tears and I don't quite know how this has become my life. My story and those of the performers have intertwined in a miraculous process of Theatre of Witness. I don't know where I end and they begin, or where tragedy and beauty meet. I know nothing. I am empty and full and I am grateful beyond belief. There is nowhere else I'd rather be, and nothing else I'd rather do. I am in love with the performers, this work, and the process. This is home for me.

CHAPTER 1

Introduction

About Theatre of Witness
and About this Book

The journey to that day backstage began in 1986 with my first Theatre of Witness production about aging. Like all of the subsequent productions, it was a full-length theatre performance created with, and performed by, the very people whose stories were being portrayed. The purpose of this form of theatre is to give voice to those who have been marginalized, forgotten, or are invisible in the larger society, and to invite audiences to bear witness to issues of suffering, redemption, and social justice. My hope is that by seeing and hearing the life stories of those who aren't often heard in our society, audience members will humanize the "other" and open their hearts and minds to the possibility of transformation.

The performers I'm continually drawn to have come through life in the extreme. They've included a refugee living in a hole in the ground and breathing through a stick of bamboo; men having spent more than 40 years in prison; women who've been homeless; former members of paramilitary organizations; families who lost loved ones to violence, and people who have committed that very violence; those who've survived war and torture; women who have come through addiction, prostitution, and domestic abuse; and a 75-year-old man living on the streets. They've been people who have come through extreme loss, despair, and grief with their spirits whole and intact, people living with deep remorse who have searched their souls and taken actions of accountability and reconciliation, and people who have found the power of love and forgiveness.

Theatre of Witness performers have become my teachers and given me inspiration and courage to live my life more boldly and fully. They've taught me how to endure and be intimate with suffering. They've taught me patience. They've taught me to hold paradox and impossibility. They've taught me how to live with joy and gratitude.

It is hard to hear the stories that come out of Theatre of Witness without reflecting on one's own life. For me, Theatre of Witness has been more than the art form I practice, the way I do social or community service, a form of political expression or an educational tool. The stories and presence of the people I work with help me understand loss and renewal in my own life. Through their stories, I learn about the universality of the human condition. I practice this art form in order to become a more conscious and loving human being. This book is a chronicle of that creative journey, a guide for those interested in pursuing this work, and a vehicle for bringing some of the participants' stories to a larger audience of readers. At the end of the book, I illuminate the Theatre of Witness guiding principles in more depth.

My Own Early Story

Growing up as an upper middle-class Jewish girl during the 1950s in suburban Boston, there was a paucity of stories. My life, although filled with family, love, and plenty, was devoid of difference and suffering. I knew little beyond the boundaries of our protected extended family and neighbors. Three of my grandparents had made the journey to America from "the old country," yet we rarely if ever heard stories of their lives in the *shtetls* of Russia and Poland, nor were told anything about their parents or grandparents. It was as if we all sprouted full-grown, like a newly mowed lawn, in a Jewish suburban homeland. And I wanted deeper roots.

My father, who'd grown up during the depression, wanted nothing more than to make a secure life for his family. So we grew up in a home where being comfortable was of paramount importance. Almost all of my parents' friends were Jewish, and almost all lived much as we did. I found myself chafing at the insularity and yearned to find my place in the larger world. I was curious about the stories of the people whose lives were somewhat invisible to me. I felt connected to people of other races and backgrounds. I wanted to hear stories about the men who worked in my father's factory or the people who came to clean our house. Their lives seemed more interesting to me than those of my family and friends.

This comfortable home brought me a vague sense of dissatisfaction. Looking back, I would say that I was starved for the raw, real, wild, and symbolic, and I yearned for spiritual connection. But luckily I had dance and skiing. As early as age four, dance became the path I used to connect with spirit and imagination. I felt myself transfixed as the music played and I "prayed with my body" to God. In many ways, it was my native tongue. Through my dance teachers, I was inspired by women who displayed inner authority and centeredness. When they pushed themselves physically, I saw a beauty and transcendence that I didn't see reflected in the lives of my mother and her mahjong and shopping friends. These female dancers became my models, and I followed in their footsteps, majoring in dance at Bennington College, which in the late 1960s was a hotbed of creative experimentation. There I learned how to make dances, how to push past the boundaries of safety, and how to work with imagery and manifest the invisible.

When I was ten, our family built a small chalet in New Hampshire, where we spent every weekend of the ski season. I loved skiing down the mountain, the cool air racing past my face as I carved wide, flowing turns through the snow. I met my boyfriend Billy in a ski-line, as he laughingly offered pickle juice straight from the jar to all of us. He and I once climbed our mountain on New Year's Eve by moonlight, leaving brightly colored M&M's on the white snow as a reminder of our path. We walked barefoot in the snow at the top, and sang at the top of our lungs all the way down. Billy taught me about the Buddha, took me to Bergman films, and initiated me into my first foray into consciousness expanding with LSD. He taught me about love, and after we broke up and I was married to someone else, he confessed that he was gay. It only made our connection even stronger. His death from AIDS years later, though tragic, was a true teaching about the power of dying with consciousness and love.

During my senior year in college, in order to move beyond the confines of the artistic world I was in, I began spending time with an old man who lived in the off-campus apartment below mine. He seemed lonely and starved for contact and conversation, so I found myself going downstairs regularly to listen to him. He told me ordinary stories about his life. But they were stories of an old man, different from the ones I heard from young artists and students. I found myself fascinated with the poetic way he spoke of his life and dreams. His physical gestures fascinated me. I didn't know it then, but the seeds for listening to people's stories were finally being watered.

Meditation came into my life through a "chance" encounter. While driving home from college one day, I picked up a hitchhiker (in those days when it seemed safe). I don't think I ever even learned his name, and he'll never know how he changed the course of my life. But there was a quality about him that touched something deep in me. He seemed peaceful and centered and spoke about being a meditator. Our conversation inspired me to try it too. So in 1972, I began a meditation practice that's been at the very center of my life. I've studied and immersed myself in TM, Buddhist, and Kabbalistic practices, going on silent retreats and studying ancient practices with wonderful and wise teachers. Without meditation I never would have had the capacity to investigate, listen, observe, and bear witness. I probably wouldn't understand how to hold opposites, how to practice compassion, and how to stay steady in the face of great suffering. I have tremendous gratitude for my living teachers who have given so freely and generously of their time and wisdom, and for those whose teachings have been passed on for generations.

After college, I married the man I had loved since age 18, and continued to dance. I performed and taught dance at Swarthmore College and studied with my mentor, Dan Wagoner, in New York. But I yearned to have children, and once I got pregnant with my oldest son, I knew that I'd eventually stop dancing myself and would therefore want to stop teaching. So I decided to get my masters degree in counseling, not sure how I would use it, but drawn to a sense of possibility. This is where this book begins.

CHAPTER 2

Growing Old is About the Growing

Aging

PHOTO © PATENTED PHOTOS

First Theatre of Witness Impulse

The first Theatre of Witness production seed was planted when, as a dancer and new mother, I decided to choreograph a dance to an audio track of my three-month-old son Daniel laughing and squealing with delight, mixed with my 88-year-old grandfather talking about getting old and meeting his great-grandson for the first time. I found the audio narrative much more compelling than the actual dance, and felt the spark of a new idea about to ignite. I decided that I wanted to explore aging by making a theatre production with old people sharing their own life stories. I knew nothing about theatre then, and in fact, very little about aging. I'd never taken a theatre class, and I knew very few old people. Yet I did know how to make dances, I did have passion, and I wasn't afraid of not knowing what I was doing. So it was the perfect place to begin.

Years

I began *Years* in 1985 by putting an advertisement in the local paper asking for older people to form a group to explore aging with me. Two men and four women appeared, and together over a few months we worked with imagery, story, movement, music, drawing, and improvisation. I interviewed them all individually and then brought them together in a group to engage in the creative process. I had them draw self-portraits and lifelines, make masks, sing songs from their younger days, play with imagery, dance, and talk about the trajectories of their lives. It was fabulously interesting to me and I began to fall in love with them. I applied for and was awarded a grant to make an interdisciplinary theatre production, and through the Pennsylvania Arts Council was introduced to playwright Rebecca Ransom. At that time, I didn't think I had the skills to write a script and was grateful to collaborate with a playwright. She and I worked closely together as she wrote the script from the material I'd gleaned in the interviews and early creative workshops. Composer and musician Heath Allen joined our team. He wrote beautiful original music, sung by the performers, based on their words and stories. Together we launched Theatre of Witness, and I invited some of the original workshop participants to become performers and held auditions to engage a few more.

Aging with Strength and Grace

There's no way for me to talk about *Years* without introducing two of the amazing women who were in it. The first, Abby Enders, was 83 when we began, and was a fixture in town, riding her bike and carrying it single-handedly up the long stairway entrance to the college. A small woman, no more than about five feet, one inch or so, she was a vibrant firebrand. At one early rehearsal we were discussing the way homes had been heated back when the participants were children. Folks were talking about wood-burning stoves and Abby repeated the respected old saying, "Well, wood warms you twice, once when you chop it and once when you burn it." I asked her if she ever chopped wood and she said, "All the time." I asked her to bring some in and one day she carried in a huge log and an ax. With tremendous body knowledge and confidence, she wielded the ax over her head and then brought it swiftly down, splitting the log in two. We all gasped. I knew at that moment that we needed to use that image in the production, if for no other reason than that no one who saw Abby split the wood could ever be tempted to say "little old lady" again. She broke all the stereotypes. The chopping of wood and telling of stories around the fire became symbols we used throughout the show, accompanied by a wonderful musical refrain composed by Heath Allen:

> Ashes to ashes, dust to dust.
> The fires of our youth have gathered a crust.
> The memories cling, in a way that we trust.
> We hold the ashes,
> We hold the dust
> Ashes to ashes...
>
> Rebecca Ransom and Heath Allen

I first heard about Kate Wright from a friend who told me of this powerful, 83-year-old activist who was living in Swarthmore. She'd been featured in a local paper, and after reading the article, I was inspired and asked her if she'd be willing to audition for *Years*. I'll never forget how she strode up to the video camera to answer the questions I'd posed about aging. "Growing old is about the growing," she said with clarity and grace. I was totally hooked. It turned out that Kate had volunteered with Vista (like the Peace Corps) after becoming a widow, and was still taking courses at Swarthmore College in her eighties and nineties. One of the most poignant moments in the show was when she and Helen, also a widow, sat in rockers onstage, each in their own world, as Helen sang and Kate spoke about the death of their husbands.

> ...When my husband died
> I felt like only half a person
> I had to weave a way to find my whole-personness again
> The right threads were not always easy to find
> And some of the ones I used to weave amazed me...
>
> [*Sung:*]
> He was a part of me
> I was a part of him
> And I liked myself as I was then
> Now I hold part of him deep within me
> And I'm growing in a brand new way.
>
> Words and music by Heath Allen

Kate and I continued to work together in two subsequent productions: *Home Tales*, and then, just before she died at age 91, *Growing up Female*. She became my inspiration and muse. Whenever I need encouragement, I still see her shining eyes and enveloping smile. I always say that I create Theatre of Witness so I can learn life lessons from the performers. One of the many lessons I learned from Kate is that it's never too late to try something new. When we were working on *Growing up Female*, she was 91, and was studying physics because, as she said, "I want to learn the laws of the universe before I die." I still don't know why she was also taking a course on feminism and pornography, but I'm sure her perspective was a tremendous and provocative addition to the class.

The first night that *Years* was performed, I watched it from the tech booth and heard lots of sniffles and blowing of noses. I incorrectly assumed that people in the audience had all come down with colds, and it wasn't until the vociferous standing ovation that I realized people had been crying. It was the biggest audience reaction there ever had been to anything I'd created up to that point, and I realized that this new form of performance had more potency than anything I'd been able to make choreographically. I still wasn't sure what had made *Years* so powerful. I thought that perhaps it was only a by-product of putting fabulously interesting people onstage playing themselves. And in a sense I was right. But as I continued to experiment with the form, I realized that this was the perfect marriage of my interests and skills, and it now felt like a calling. Two theatre productions later, in 1991, I left my dance faculty position, metaphorically jumped off the cliff, and started a non-profit company, TOVA—"Artistic Projects for Social Change," through which I could continue doing this work. I still didn't know what name to use in referring to this new art form though, and it wasn't until a few years later that it suddenly came to me: Theatre of Witness.

CHAPTER 3

I Make Myself at Home Wherever I Am

Homelessness

One of the more difficult years of my life was 1991. Alone, with two young children, I was grieving both the death of my father (and second parent to die), and an unexpected divorce. The aloneness was dark, endless, and primordial. In the midst of it, I was struggling to understand where and what home was. To whom did I belong? Who belonged to me? This deep questioning fostered a desire in me to hear and learn from other people who'd lost their home. I decided to make a Theatre of Witness piece about homelessness, hoping that if I immersed myself in their stories, then perhaps I'd find my own way home.

As always, when the impulse comes to begin a project, I try to put myself into a receptive state of grace, where I begin to pay exquisite attention to details, images, and dreams I have. I watch who shows up in my life and what synchronistic moments occur. I observe when I feel excited and moved by an encounter or idea. Oftentimes I pray for guidance. All of these modes of awareness came into play when the Morales family and I crossed paths.

Sofia and Carlos

I was at a Friday night Sabbath service at a synagogue when I first met Carlos. He and his wife Sofia had recently arrived from El Salvador and were living in political sanctuary. Speaking to the congregation with deep conviction, Carlos asked us if we'd support him in a five-day fast and vigil in response to the assassination of Archbishop Romero, known as the "Bishop of the Poor" in San Salvador. I was greatly moved by Carlos's story, but perhaps even more by something in his bearing. He was someone with an inner authority, who had committed his life to the struggle for justice. He was someone who'd been torn from his homeland and was trying to make a new home in a new culture. I immediately signed on to be a volunteer driver for him, hoping it would bring me a bit closer to this extraordinary man.

At the end of his vigil, I got up the courage to ask Carlos if he and Sofia would be willing to be in the Theatre of Witness project I was just beginning—*Home Tales*. Without understanding what he was committing to, he said they would. In fact, he asked if his three children could also be part of the project.

Onstage, Carlos shared his story of being a union organizer and activist in El Salvador. He spoke about the suffering of his people, the disappeared, the juntas, and the death threats he received. He spoke about his decision to risk everything, leaving his three children behind while he and Sofia escaped across the desert to come to the United States in the hopes of claiming sanctuary and eventually sending for their children. Their story of crossing the desert, with grown men on their hands and knees sucking water from mud, was heartbreaking and harrowing (see Chapter 10). They were captured, beaten, and sent to a refugee camp. Eventually they were reunited with their children, but their struggle to make a new home in a new land, culture, and language was just as overwhelming as their escape. The whole story was laden with trauma and epic in proportion.

I learned many things by working with the Morales family. Most important, I was deeply inspired by their strength. My own losses seemed so manageable compared to what they'd gone through. I witnessed the inner strength of their conviction, their willingness to share their vulnerability with each other and with us, and their courage to make extraordinary changes in their lives.

I also learned what it was like to work with people recovering from trauma. Although they were now safe in the United States, Sofia and Carlos each still harbored deep and sometimes open wounds. There were days, as they told their stories, when there were many tears, and sometimes also anger between them. I watched Sofia struggle to express herself in a new language, and I learned to give her the space to find her own way. As a director, I had to let the content of their story, as well as the depth of emotion that they revealed, move me, but not shake me. I had to become a pillar strong enough for them to feel safe to relive their trauma, knowing I could hold whatever would emerge. For them to trust me, I had to trust myself and I had to find my own center and stability. It was also important that the family was in psychotherapy and had a large support community in the political sanctuary movement. Their therapist supported our work together, and I felt we were all safer in mining such deep material.

When we rehearsed the scene about them leaving their home and children, it became clear that reliving the memory reactivated old wounds between them. I knew I had to script it so they had some leeway to follow the emotional truth emerging in the moment. So I wrote it so that, if Sofia felt great anger, she could stomp off ahead of Carlos, displaying her rage and grief alone. Other times, when they were immersed in their sorrow, they could hug before walking offstage hand in hand.

I learned also how important it was for me to find a personal and yet universal image in everyone's story. Even though our backgrounds couldn't have been more dissimilar, I was deeply connected to the father–daughter relationship demonstrated by Carlos and his daughter Alicia, age 16. Like other teens of that age in the United States, she was struggling with her desire for autonomy and for the freedom to date boys. Carlos was trying to hold on to the values and cultural norms of his homeland and yet adapt to the social expectations here. In many ways, their love and the push–pull of her desire for individuation reminded me of my own relationship with my father before he died.

In directing Alicia, my first impulse was to have her do her part alone, or with another performer her own age, so that she'd feel free to express the full range of her feeling. To that end, I tried many different scenarios, none of which seemed to capture the emotion or tone. Then I asked her if she would be willing to explore doing her scene with her father. When I brought them together in the studio, I asked them if they ever danced together, with Alicia's feet standing on Carlos's, as I had often done with my own father. They had. We improvised their scene that way, and tears abounded as Carlos finally said to her, "I know that someday you will grow up and leave. But I want you to know that I'll always be here for you. Always." Every time I saw that scene of tenderness between them, for more than the full year that we toured the production, my eyes would fill up. Their physical intimacy evoked a flood of loss and longing for my own dad. The scale of the Morales family's story was huge in magnitude, and yet the familiar struggles of fathers and daughters everywhere is much of what resonated for many of us in the audience. It humanized what might have been too big a story to drink in.

Michael

When I was casting the production of *Home Tales*, I knew that I wanted to bring together a diverse set of people who experienced homelessness in a variety of contexts. To find possible participants I did what I call the "casting of the net." I set the intention to find people and opened myself to the receptive state of grace. And then I networked like crazy. I met with social workers, immigrant specialists, university faculty, and with anyone who offered a lead of any kind.

In addition to the Morales family, performers included two refugees from Vietnam, a mother and son who'd lived in the projects, an older woman deciding whether to go into a nursing home, a young boy moving between his two divorced parents, and a 75-year-old white man living on the streets. All of them had dealt with leaving home, or maybe a better way to describe it is that home left them.

A theatre director I knew told me about Michael, whom he described as an amazing man living on the streets who had recently worked with this director's group. He suggested that I might find him at a senior outreach hot lunch program in North Philadelphia. I called the folks who ran the program and got their go-ahead to come in and look for him.

Michael was easy to spot. With his long, white beard, knitted cap, and jaunty walk, he was a fixture at the center. I asked someone to introduce us. I quickly noticed the twinkle in his sky-blue eyes and his openness. He carried a silver harmonica in his back pocket.

I asked if I could sit with him. Although it might sound like an everyday thing for me to meet a man who was living on the streets, it's not without shame that I admit that in fact I was fairly terrified. Of what, I'm not sure. Probably just the unknown. He was dirty. His clothes didn't match. He seemed to be someone who surely had a few mental health diagnoses, and I was afraid of his unpredictability. But probably more truthfully— he was "homeless," and my white, upper middle-class, privileged upbringing spoke words of prejudice and fear in my head. I was scared, but I squelched it all and just sat with him, listening to his rambling yet poignant stories. Slowly letting go of one fear after another.

One of the first things he said was:

> People call me homeless. But I'm not homeless.
> I make myself at home wherever I am.

I got the chills. He'd somehow succinctly spoken a gem of truth that I knew was something I wanted more than anything to learn. Here was a man who slept rough in a park every night, come snow, rain, heat, or cold, and he was content.

"*I make myself at home wherever I am.*" I believed him. It was clear that he was someone living totally in the moment. Relaxing into the flow of life. Clearly somewhat unhinged—yet perhaps a prophet. Certainly a teacher.

So I kept going back and sitting with him at lunchtime. Eventually I asked him if he'd be willing to be in the production of *Home Tales* that we were going to begin rehearsing in a town 25 miles away. He agreed, and for more than a year I drove 100 miles for every rehearsal to pick him up at the edge of the park where he slept, bring him to our rehearsal, and then drive him back. He didn't have a watch, a phone, or a home, and yet Michael never missed a rehearsal or performance. He was never even late.

Michael had incredible dignity. I believe it's essential in Theatre of Witness work that performers are paid. They sign a contract agreeing to be on time, come to all rehearsals, abide by the principles of confidentiality and respect agreed on by the group, and finish the project. The producing agency agrees to pay them an honorarium for rehearsals and performances. As did the others, Michael signed the contract, but when it came time to pay him, I had the hardest time getting him to accept his honorarium. At first I realized I'd been so unthinking in giving him a check, as he had no way to cash it. But when I tried giving him cash, he refused that too. He'd say, "Wait until the whole project is over and if you're happy with my performance, then I'll take it." I think this came from a genuine desire to please as well as to not be beholden to anyone. He always said he liked being on his own and didn't want to live in a shelter. And he seemed genuinely content with the little he had, which was mostly garbage pickings that he kept stashed in bags. He didn't want any handouts of any kind. The only way he'd accept food from us was if we'd all eat together. So we learned to bring extra sandwiches and fruit to rehearsals and we would then ask if he'd do us a favor by bringing the leftovers back to someone else who might need them.

At one very poignant moment, one of the other cast members, herself someone who lived in poverty, offered him a beautiful men's raincoat. Michael began crying and said, "I want to be the giver, not the taker." That was a profound lesson for me about dignity and the power differential between giving and receiving. And I learned to accept his gifts to me—including half-drunk miniature liquor bottles and a lamp he'd found out on the street. These were precious finds and came from his heart.

On a technical level, working with him presented a series of challenges that were quite unique. He had lost his reading glasses, and wouldn't let us replace them, so he wasn't able to read his script. He knew his own stories by heart, but the trouble always came when he went off on a tangent, or forgot an important line that was a cue for someone else. In an attempt to take the problem and turn it into the solution, I decided to put my 11-year-old son in the scene with him. Daniel sat on the ground in front of Michael with the script hidden in a *Mad* magazine which he kept flipping through, and when Michael would veer way off his lines, Daniel would turn to him and say, "Hey Michael—tell me about the..." Then Michael would delightedly tell that story as if he'd just thought of it himself. Those moments felt as if we broke through the fourth wall of the theatre, with Michael once again defining the boundaries of reality. One night in the performance Michael began talking about sleeping in a tree that was filled with crawling ants. As the story meandered, I began panicking backstage about how Daniel would ever get him back on track. Luckily he was brilliant at it, and Michael finally said his cue lines. And just in case I ever wanted to take too much credit for the success of the show, that particular night a man came over, hugged both Michael and me, and said, "The best part of the whole show was the story about those ants."

I lost track of Michael a few years after the production. During the tour, he was used to standing ovations, people surrounding him after each show, showering him with hugs and congratulations—some of the very same people who may have walked right by him out on the street. He was written about in the press and was used to being a central part of a new community. He was needed and respected, and I think that all of that wore down some of his resistance. For most people that would be a good thing, but for someone living as he did on the streets, it breached some of his well-established defenses and protection. I could see that he was more vulnerable.

So with a bit of prodding, I finally got him to accept my offer of paying for a few months' rent in a shared apartment. It didn't work out well. His first roommate called me one night, all in a dither because Michael was leaving sour milk in the refrigerator, peeing in the sink, and hanging his wet underwear on the living room lamps. I found him a second home—this time with a woman who frequented the same lunch program. She too called me less than a week later. "He has to leave. He's racist." "What makes you say that?" "He used to wear black socks or white socks, but now he's wearing one black one and one white one, and I know it means he's uncomfortable living with someone black." I thought then that before I began this work, there was no way I could have foreseen I'd be trying to negotiate my way out of a situation such as this. It was at that point that I decided I'd better bow out and let him continue to make his own choices. I don't think Michael wanted to be domesticated. He was able to be self-sufficient, making his home in the park. But making a home within someone else's norms and expectations was too much for him. At that point, the line between my ethical responsibility to "fix his life" and his need for freedom and autonomy clashed, and I realized that I needed to respect his decisions and lifestyle. Regardless of his unusual way of living, who was I to presume that living another way would be best for him? I realized then that although it may take me the rest of my life, if I could learn the lesson from him, *"I make myself at home wherever I am,"* I might possibly have one of the big keys to happiness. Over 20 years later, I am still working on it.

CHAPTER 4

Death is an Everyday Thing

Refugees and Immigrants

Between the Crack

In 1992 I was invited by the Painted Bride Art Center in Philadelphia to meet with a group of Vietnamese refugee teens in Southwest Philadelphia. The invitation followed what had been a racially motivated killing in a city park. Harry Reilly, an 18-year-old white teen, had been stabbed to death as he tried to break up a fight between white and Vietnamese young men. Prosecutors had charged six Vietnamese teens with murder in the first degree. Huang Tran, a wonderful community worker, was looking for methods to help other Vietnamese teens deal with their feelings and tell their stories. The Painted Bride suggested they meet with me.

At our first meeting, Huang, five teenage boys, and I met in a small dark room. Some of the boys spoke English, others didn't. I remember wondering if any of them would want to engage with me—a middle-age white, Jewish woman who lived in the suburbs. I wasn't sure where to begin.

So I asked them to tell me what was going on in their lives. Quickly they spoke about racial attacks and being targeted and picked up by the police on an almost daily basis. I asked them what the police said to them. "They say they want to know who we are." The police would then take them to the station, photograph them, and then put their pictures into a mugshot book. After that, victims, looking through the pictures, could easily identify the teens as potential crime suspects. This was an illegal abuse of justice. But as refugees and teens, the young men felt powerless. I knew that, with this revelation, we had "found the gold in the story." It would give me some place to hang my hat thematically. At the end of our meeting, four of them decided to join the project. Later, one dropped out and was replaced by his sister. Together we created one of the first scenes:

[*A white policeman comes to the school and Jerry, a Vietnamese teen, is called to meet him in the conference room.*]

P: Sit down Jerry. I just want to talk with you a minute. You probably heard about the robbery last week. I just want to find out what you know about it. We know that it was some Vietnamese boys that did it. So, Jerry…if you cooperate it would be very good.

J: I don't know anything about it. I heard it was a Chinese gang.

P: Ah. So you know something about it Jerry.

J: No. It's just what I heard. I don't know anything about it.

P: Are you sure Jerry? Are you sure? I can't tell whether you're telling the truth. Maybe if I take you to the station that would help you remember.

[*They go downstage left. Jerry is downstage and the policeman keeps asking him to turn in order to take photos from a few angles.*]

P: So Jerry, maybe you can help us identify some pictures.

[*He takes him upstage where the rest of the cast is lined up. One by one, they step into line.*]

P: Well thanks Jerry. I'm sorry about that. I appreciate your help. I'd really like to be friends. I'd like to know more about your culture. Can you teach me a few words in Vietnamese?
Like what's the word for "fuck" Jerry?

Once I heard about the mugshots, I knew that we could turn this potent negative image into something positive. To that end, we had beautiful, large, black-and-white photo portraits commissioned of each of the performers and placed them onstage. Those gorgeous and haunting pictures of their faces, the very antithesis of police mugshots, became the "medicine" in the show. We then used the cop's query as the path into the stories about their lives:

…The cops say they want to know who we are.
They don't know anything about us.
If they really want to know us, they'd ask us about our lives.
Our dreams. Our past.
They'd ask us about our lives back in Vietnam.
About the land, the war, our journeys.
They'd ask us what we feel and think.
They'd ask us what is in the inside.

The more I got to know the teens, the more moved I became by their strength—and passion. These were young adults who as children had crossed oceans in rickety boats, who'd fled pirates and the war, and who were the first English speakers in their families. They were dealing with the intense pressure of family cultural expectations, daily doses of racism, and trying to make it in a new language and new land where they felt unwelcome. They'd lived more in their short 16 years than I had in my 42.

Bao:

…In Saigon I remember one day they bombed the town and some people were killed.
A lot of other people went to see what had happened and then another bomb came and killed them.
My father told me to stay away from there. I got used to it.
I wasn't scared 'cause my father was there.
I've seen so many dead bodies. It doesn't affect me anymore.
It's an everyday thing.
There were dead people all the time in my village.
Killed by the Viet Cong.
And I've seen people killed by gunshot here.
Sometimes I can't determine how I feel.
Death is an everyday thing…

Jerry:

…We were on the ocean for nine days and nights.
We were out of food and water.
One woman died.
My sister gave birth to a new girl…
They named her Te Jung, which means ocean.
It was all very mystical.
On the boat I was the calmest.
Me and my grandma were the two calmest.
I remember the waves. It was like a seesaw.
I thought it was going to cut my boat in half.

On the ocean Death is so near—it's like a turn of the hand.
You don't worry about morals
or throwing up or going to the bathroom.
People start praying. Praying for acceptance.

Lan:

My brothers and sisters don't remember much about
our lives in Vietnam.
They don't remember a lot that happened to us when we escaped.
My brother was about five—I was six.
Some things in our lives are too terrible to keep in our heads.
They don't remember—but I do...

From there, Lan described the night they left, with everyone pushing to get on the boat, the hiding of gold in the pipes of the boat, and her fear and illness on the boat.

There were pirates everywhere!
We saw them swimming through the water with dark knives in their mouths. They had bandanas around their heads.
They were getting closer and closer!
The pirates wanted money and pretty women.
I remember them asking my brother if he had any money.
He pulled out a nickel—he was crying,
"This is all I have—please take it."
But they laughed at him—a little boy—
they wanted gold and pretty girls.
My aunt was crying to her Mom to help her—"They want me!"
Her Mom grabbed her and hid her under a blanket.
All the girls put grease and oil on their faces to look ugly so they wouldn't get captured.
My other aunt had a mud face and grabbed her brother,
"This is my husband!"
I put grease on my face too.
They got two sisters. One of them jumped overboard.
They kept the other one for a while—we heard she survived.
I was crying, and very scared.
The pirates took apart our engine and they found the gold.
Then they threatened us.
If we didn't give them everything they would take us back into the middle of the ocean and leave us there...

The first time we performed *Between the Crack* was a year to the day after the killing in the city park. The trial was in full swing, and we were inundated by the press. The evening performance was held in the auditorium of one of the schools close to the park, and because we were extremely worried about reprisals and violence, we arranged for security. None of us knew what might be unleashed.

That evening, there was a full house of audience members: young and old; white; black; and Vietnamese. Huang Tran introduced the show in Vietnamese and English. The performers were strong and powerful and there was a long, standing ovation at the end. Then, as they lined up across the stage for their bow, a young African American teen jumped up onto the stage. I was startled with fear and wondered if this might indicate the beginning of some kind of violent altercation. From where I was sitting, I couldn't see, but behind this young man's back was a bouquet of azaleas. He handed them to Jerry. Jerry held them briefly, smiled, shook the young man's hand, and then in a poignant gesture of grace and peace, gave the flowers back to him. It was a spontaneous and beautiful moment of connection, so real and unexpected that it still remains one of my most favorite moments in 25 years of Theatre of Witness.

It wasn't only that first performance that gave us all a fright. When we next performed *Between the Crack* for 1,000 inner-city high-school students, their initial reactions almost made me pull the curtain and stop the show. Imagine the scene—a vast school auditorium filled with noisy students being yelled at by teachers patrolling the aisles, "Get in your seat. Hands to yourself!" The intimacy and delicacy of the stories were completely at odds with the frenetic energy in this venue. My heart sank.

We could still hear laughing and talking in the audience after the show began. Then, in one of the early scenes in which the performers spoke about being called "Chink," students began shouting epithets and taunting the performers. I was horrified and didn't know what to do. This was the exact opposite of anything I ever wanted for Theatre of Witness. We do this work in order to reduce prejudice and separation, not to inflame it, and my instinct was to protect the performers from this abuse by turning off the lights and stopping the show. But before I could get to the technical staff, I noticed that the performers were just continuing on as if nothing untoward was happening. Jerry continued with poise:

> Sometimes I feel like a mouse.
> I have my own life to live and someone else doesn't like it.
> Someone wants to get rid of you.
> Like a cockroach.
> That's why I never kill the cockroach.

Then after another short scene, Jerry began singing a song he'd written. It wasn't the actual words that were powerful—it was the simplicity of this gentle melody and the vulnerability of his delivery. He sang about the feelings that "ran deep inside of him" in a way that somehow reached the students. You could hear a pin drop in the auditorium. I still don't know why it all turned so quickly—whether it was Jerry's mixture of quietness and strength, or whether it was his centeredness, but something in the room shifted, and from then on, the performers had the audience's undivided attention. There was a long, standing ovation at the end. For me, this turnaround was an act of grace and a demonstration of the power of Theatre of Witness. I believe we all hunger for something real and truthful, and, when we see it, can become disarmed.

Between the Crack was the first total immersion I had into the stories and lives of refugees and it propelled me into further Theatre of Witness work with refugees and immigrants from places such as Cambodia, Russia, Sudan, Pakistan, Poland, Brazil, Palestine, and, once again, Vietnam. The stories of these performers were about the violent wrenching away of home, country, language, family, and identity. These were similar themes to ones I've been working with my whole life. But in these cases the stories were vastly more dramatic and tragic. For a witness or audience, the losses endured by these storytellers were often almost too big to contain. But raw and tragic as so many of these stories were, I have always come away totally humbled by the resilience displayed by the performers I've met. They've taught me about the power of the human spirit to overcome what seems unbearable beyond our comprehension. This was especially true with the Cambodian teens in *Children of Cambodia / Children of War.*

Children of Cambodia

I was surprised, when I met the inner-city Cambodian teens, at how much they remembered about their lives back home, and how deeply embedded the dances, music, and customs were. This was very different from my experience with the Vietnamese teens, who'd had only very fragmented memories of their homeland. Their collective memories had centered around their journeys from Vietnam and their lives in the United States trying to adjust to American culture. The cast of *Children of Cambodia*, however, had numerous common memories of life under the Khmer Rouge, as well as ancient rituals passed down through the generations. They wanted to integrate these customs and images within the storytelling. Artistically, it was one of the more satisfying projects I worked on, as we were able to fully use props and movement as an integral part of the storytelling. Translucent white voile cloth became "the spirit of Cambodia," as well as wind, water, and shrouds. Traditional Cambodian fighting sticks were used, not only to showcase the partnered dance form but also as shovels, walking sticks, guns, prods, water-carrying poles, and abstract shapes in dance imagery. We used them all in Chenda's story—a story almost too unbearable to hear:

> It's 1975. I am six years old and live in the city.
> We heard on the radio that we were going to have a new leader—
> Pol Pot.
> Then I heard the shooting. The Khmer Rouge walked on the street.
> They say "Get out of your house or you'll be killed!"
> To prove it, on the fourth day, they burn a house
> with people still inside.
> One day we travel on the road into the jungle.
> We have no house, no roof. We live in the field.
> The Khmer Rouge give each person one square meter of plastic.
> We sleep on the ground.
> The plastic becomes our roof in the rain.

Next they start to collect all the children under the age of 12.
They take us to the children's camp.
There is not enough food, no medicine either.
Each morning they wake us at 4:30.
At 12 noon we each get one spoon of rice and a banana.
Then we work till 6:30 at night.
We get the same thing to eat again, plus one teaspoon of salt.
After one year I decide to escape with three of my friends.
We walk all night until we find our family,
but only my mother and one sister is left.
They'd accused my father of being a soldier and they moved him
to another mobile unit.
The day I came home, he'd asked permission to come home and
the Khmer met him for the first time.
I am upstairs and the Khmer Rouge soldiers come in and
call my father's name.
I don't know how they know my father is at home.
They come with a horse and say they are going to take my father
to have a meeting in another village.
And I know what is going to happen.
I say I'm going to follow them.
They put my father in front of the horse and
I keep running after them.
Suddenly they stop the horse.
My father turn back and say "Where is the meeting?"
They say "You can pray now before you die."
Then they tell him to dig a hole for himself.
He digs.
After a while they say he can step in the hole.
My father step inside the hole and they say
"You can pray before you die."
"Please when you go back to the village don't tell my wife and
children I die. Just tell my wife to take care of my children."
I just listen.
I want to get out, to go with my father,
but I hold myself and lie on the ground.
I say "No—my father is going to be OK."
They kill him with a stick.
My father fall into the hole and die.
They laugh…

Onstage, one of the performers slowly dug his own grave with one of the sticks. Then the other young men took it from him and, in a slow motion arc, smoothly brought it to the back of his neck as he fell to the ground. Later, portraying the marches of escape through the jungles, they circled the stage with sticks.

> Keep walking, that's the only way to live.
> If we stay in one place, we die.

> The Khmer Rouge say all the educated have to be killed.
> They destroy the Temple.

> We know we have to keep on walking, or else they will kill us.

> With one handful of rice we have to feed the whole family.
> I was sick and hungry.

> We walk through jungles. Sometimes we stay in people's houses.
> But when we hear the shootings, we run.

> Everywhere we went, people were looking for their children.

> We walked through rivers and deserts. People step on mines.
> Their legs are cut off.

> One of the bombs dropped on the temple
> and cuts off the Buddha's head.

> They wipe the blood of the people on the Buddha's body.

> We pass the bones of those who died.
> The bones pile up as high as the mountains.

Later in the show, the sticks were used to turn and push dead bodies into mass graves. The white voile was used to cover them in shrouds. It is imagery that still haunts me to this day and reminds me of something an audience member said about a later Theatre of Witness production in Northern Ireland: "It's beauty born from ugliness." I think in some ways that's the artistic edge. How do we take something so horrific and without diluting the terribleness, make it into something we as audience members can hold and bear?

But perhaps the most inhumane and almost unbelievable story was Chenda's story of living for a year and a half in a hole in the ground in a refugee camp in Thailand. To tell it, we played an audiotape of her voice mixed with music. She sat onstage amidst suspended voile cloth, as if in a hole, and slowly moved her hands and head towards the sky.

> I live in a hole in the ground. If I'm found they'll report me and
> send me back to Cambodia, where I'll be killed.
> I live under the ground. There is mud and it is very cold.
> I breathe through a stick of bamboo.
> If someone takes the bamboo away, I will die.
> There is a neighbor who gives me food.
> I'm hungry all the time. I can't move. I sleep sitting up.
> All the time I tell myself, I say
> "Chenda you will survive.
> You have to go through this hard time
> but then you will have a better future."
> I pray a lot. I dream of a soft mattress and food.
> I live in the hole for one and a half years.

Like all those refugees onstage, she did survive. She survived, but has indelible memories of so many who didn't. And it is to honor their memory that so many performers have felt compelled to tell these stories. They tell them to heal for themselves, yes, but more so, to honor the dead, to educate those who don't know, and to remember themselves.

Six Points of the Star

> In Russia everyone had a passport marked with five points of
> identification. The fifth point was nationality. If you had "Jewish"
> written in the fifth point, it was like having a defect or a disability.

One of the most challenging projects I worked on was *Six Points of the Star* with Jewish Russian refugees who had left Russia in the 1980s and 1990s due to anti-Semitism. The performers were all wonderful people with powerful and sad stories.

> My remembrances start during the war.
> Leningrad 1942 I am four years old.
> The war has started and all hopes have finished.
> There is blockade. Our single city. No way to get in or out.

There is no food. No heat.
People start to be very hungry. We can no longer receive money—
only a voucher—a very restricted amount for bread.
People start to die from hunger.

Before the war my mother always tried to feed me, but when the
war started she remembers me in only one pose—
on my bed with my hand out.
I no longer smile.
I just say, "Feed me."
All the food that my mother receives
she gives to my grandfather and me.
She starts to lose weight. In one year she weighs only 75 pounds.
She now looks like a small boy.

We suffer from the cold. The winter is very strong
and we have to heat ourselves by burning our furniture.
During this winter there is much ice on Ladishka Lake.
And only a single road to get in or out.
This road is called the "Road to Life."
It is the edge between life and death.

We are hungry and are going to starve.
My mother decides to leave her parents and take me with her
through the Road to Life.
There are many German planes and a lot of bombs.
We travel by truck and then transfer to train to Siberia.
All the other children on the train very envy me
because my mother always feeds me any food she has.
Then she loses consciousness and is transferred to a hospital.

People take me off the train and bring me to a special home for
children with no parents.
All the time I ask that I wait for my Mama.
I stand by the rear window entire months, waiting for my Mama.
Finally they move my bed there and let me sleep and eat by that
window, waiting.

My mother's body was already in the morgue.
But she wanted to stay alive because of me.
She asks for 40 cups of water to clean out the poisons from hunger.
And she starts to live. She gets healthier every hour, every day.

When my mother gets better she comes to the home of her father.
They send for me.
My mother said that when she saw me
I had no longer the face of a child.
I was three years old and I have the face of a very old woman.
I cry when I have my mother so close to me.
The very old woman and her small boy mother.

The stories of these Jewish Russian refugees, like the performers themselves, were strong. They'd lived through war, hunger, and Chernobyl. More recently they'd also lived under communism, where waiting in long lines for meager rations of food was a way of life. They'd learned how to assert themselves and fight for whatever they could get. While these power struggles had obviously served them well in the Soviet Union, that same behavior in rehearsal was a surprise and a bit upsetting to me. I still remember one day trying to direct one of the performers when she looked at me and said: "I refuse." I tried to find out why she refused, and she stood with her arms crossed, looking at one of the other performers: "He thinks I look funny, so I refuse to do it." I had to get our composer, singer Natasha Jitormaskaia, also from Kiev, to intervene on my behalf. Whenever the performers thought I didn't know what I was doing (which was often), they'd revert to Russian and begin arguing their case to Natasha, who'd then mediate between us. I knew on some fundamental level that they couldn't see my vision of what the finished production would be like once it was all put together, and they were scared. They would complain to Natasha in Russian, often leaving me totally unable to understand anything they were saying. It was hard work for all of us.

Then, as we began to weave the parts of the production together, they began to feel a bit more confident. But it wasn't until after the first performance, when they were met with a standing ovation, that they really felt they could stand behind the work. One by one, each of them later apologized to me, saying that they hadn't been able to see what I had seen. I thought I understood this phenomenon, but it wasn't until years later when working on *Beyond the Walls*, when the shoe was on the other foot, that I truly knew what they'd experienced.

I was collaborating with film-maker Rachel Libert on a filmed section for the *Beyond the Walls* production. She was shooting images to correspond to the text and music already written about the decline and violence of inner-city neighborhoods. One of the images Rachel suggested using was of hands slowly falling off the bars of a Jungle Gym. I thought her idea sounded hokey and I was somewhat ambivalent. Then I accompanied her to the film shoot in the playground and I even looked through the camera lens as she filmed people's hands sliding off the bars. Rachel explained to me how she planned to slow the images down in the edit and use sepia tones. Even watching the filming myself, I still didn't think it would work, although I was willing to wait and see what the finished result was.

Then, when I saw the film put together, I was totally blown away. It was absolutely breathtaking. Her imagery was perfect and totally complemented the words and music. It was only then that I realized that, even though she'd carefully explained her vision to me and in fact I'd even watched her film it, I hadn't been able to see what she was imagining. Unable to envision what she saw, I had doubts. I realized it was the same process that had happened between the performers and me in *Six Points of the Star*. It requires a leap of faith for performers to trust that I'm steering us towards something worthwhile, even when I do my best to translate my vision for them. It takes an even bigger leap of faith for a group of immigrants or refugees to trust an outsider director with the essence of their imagery and to trust that their stories will be well translated. I now have great respect for the magnitude of this act, and I'm quite humbled by it.

CHAPTER 5

These Hands

Women and Girls

Daughters of Connection

Growing up Female was perhaps one of the lighter projects I've worked on. Instead of relying on dark stories of war and resettlement, we were attempting to discover the answer to a question: What does it mean to grow up female from the perspective of girls and women of African American, white, Latina, and Asian backgrounds? We brought together a large and diverse group of women and girls from ages 8 to 91, and together we created and modeled an intergenerational community of sisterhood.

Something magical happened. The young girls, teenagers, adults, and older women created a sacred container, and their stories poured out with tears and laughter. *Growing up Female* was a large and sometimes unwieldy production, but underneath all the particular details of the stories, we uncovered a sense of commonality and strength in the power of being female. The stories were sorrowful, angry, questioning, and joyous. But the group held each other with great respect, love, and humor, and new and lasting relationships were formed. My job was to weave the diverse threads of their stories together into a whole.

In our early rehearsals, based on many of the interviews and discussions, I often asked the performers to work in pairs, improvising small vignettes and physically symbolizing ideas that they'd expressed. Because for the first time in my Theatre of Witness work I fit the demographic of the group, and because we didn't have an even number, I sometimes participated. There was one day when, working with Faye on body image issues, I ended up sharing a story that up until that moment I'd kept quite hidden. It was a story that I'd held in shame and secret, about having had plastic surgery on my nose at age 16. Faye and I improvised a short vignette together, during which I relived the horror of removing the bandages and seeing my new face for the first time. At that moment, I made a startling connection between my surgery and my grandmother Tessa's story about leaving her homeland at age 16. I found this link not only to be surprisingly comforting, but it transformed what had once been a shameful and terrifying memory into a larger familial story of courage and exploration. This reframing became for me what I always refer to as one of the core guiding principles of Theatre of Witness: "finding the medicine" in the story. I believe that we all have our own medicine, sometimes hidden even from ourselves, that, once tapped, can truly initiate a powerful, transformative journey of healing.

When I shared this vignette in rehearsal with the other participants, the women suggested that I perform with them in the production. At first I was resistant, being afraid that I wouldn't be able to properly direct them if I too was a performer. But then I realized that I could limit my involvement to that one scene plus the introduction and conclusion. I also realized that it was no longer fair of me to expect others to mine their deepest stories if I myself wasn't willing to experience it from the inside out. I knew it would help me understand the process better and therefore become a better support for performers. So it was then that I ended up sharing my most shameful secret with thousands of people:

I am searching for my grandmother.

I am not looking for her in the United States
or on any other continent.
I am looking for her memories and imprints
in the crevices and folds of my heart.
For she has long since died.

When Tessa Kurtzman was a 16-year-old Jewish girl
in Austria/Poland,
She left her home, her country, her people,
And sailed in steerage alone to the United States.
She carried with her the name of her sister, a ten-dollar bill,
and no English.
She carried in her suitcase courage and grace.

When I was a 16-year-old Jewish girl
in Newton, Massachusetts,
I, too, left my heritage and history.
I allowed my mother, and her friends, and doctor to convince me
to have plastic surgery on my nose.
To make me pretty.
With one final break—the sound of which I will never forget,
I let them erase generations of ancestors from my face.
I let them reshape a new nose on my now non-Jewish face.
When the bandages came off and I saw
myself for the first time in the mirror, I was horrified.
I couldn't recognize myself.
Looking back at me in the mirror was the face of a stranger.
A young girl cut from all that had come before.

My grandmother came to this country alone.
I did not know her then.

I knew her only as an old woman,
An old woman with gray hair tied back in a French twist.
Who made knadlich, and kreplach, and shared her enveloping love
that made each of her eight grandchildren *know*
that they were her most favorite.

My grandmother always wore high heels,
and had the straight back of a lady.
She smelled of apples and roses and grandmother's lap.
And I loved to watch her knit and crochet her past together with
her new family into her ample bosom.

I am now searching for the severed pieces of my Jewish past.
I am searching for my spiritual foremothers whose names
we do not know, who weren't mentioned in the stories,
and whose memories we have had to make up.
I search for women who cross oceans alone, and wander into new
lands they were never prepared to make home.

I am searching for my grandmother,
Woman of courage and grace.

Growing up Female, 1993

Never Too Late to Love

Hildegarde was a petite and beautiful 84-year-old African American woman with a contagious smile. She was a lady through and through, who'd grown up in the White House where her father had been the headwaiter under President Taft. It still seems so extraordinary that she'd ever heard about the audition. She happened to be at a garden party where someone mentioned having seen a flyer announcing that I was looking for women and girls of all ages. She was intrigued and decided to come. I do believe that miracles happen in this receptive phase of "casting the net." Sometimes all that we need is to set the intention, put out the word, and someone like Hildegarde appears. I fell in love with her immediately.

Hildegarde and Kate, who was 91 at the time, felt like elder fountains of love and blessings for the rest of us. Having their presence onstage was a constant reminder of the healing balm of love. They became inspirations for all of us younger women. This was especially so when Hildegarde told us about falling in love at age 79. Onstage she told the story as she sat with the other older women around a small tea table:

> Well this is what happened to me when I first turned 79. I met this wonderful gentleman at a dinner party. After it was over my hostess asked him "Would you drive Mrs. Robinson home?" He didn't really want to, but he was a gentleman. When we got to my house, something told me "Hilda, don't let this man get away," so I invited him in.
> "Mr. Perry, would you like to stay for a cup of coffee?"
> He said "Yes."
> "Where would you like to have it?"
> "Where do you make it?"
> "In the kitchen."
> "Then that's where we will drink it." Well, we sat for almost 8 hours, and we never touched that coffee…but we touched each other… When he got up to go again I thought
> "Don't let him get away!"
> When he went to leave he asked if he could give me a kiss.
> I said "yes" and went to put my face up but just when he bent over, I put my hand over my mouth!
> "What—beautiful and shy?"
> I wasn't shy. My dentures had slipped!

As it happens sometimes, this story was scripted word for word from a question I'd posed the group about sexuality. Hildegarde had blurted out, "I still see a gynecologist," and then we'd all dissolved into howls of laughter. There was something so whole-heartedly warm and surprising in her embarrassment at having disclosed this. Hildegarde constantly reminded us that age was just a state of mind, in an upbeat and delightful song she sang and danced to:

> Just a three letter word called "Age"
> Just a three letter word called "Age"
> You say I can't do it—I'm too old.
> You say I can't dance,
> My bones have grown cold.

You say I can't love,
My heart is dead.
Well let me tell you
It's all in your head.

I can walk, I can dance,
With a heart for romance.
I can walk, I can dance…

Hildegarde developed deep grandmotherly friendships with many of the cast members, as well as with me. It was hard to hold fast to the boundaries that I usually keep with the performers in her presence—she was just too loving. I remember one day when the cast was at my house for a party. In my personal life I was still quite angry at my second husband, from whom I was divorced, and must have expressed it somewhat forcibly. Hildegarde took me aside and, with a loving but penetrating gaze, said, "Hate only hurts the heart of the one who hates. I want you to repeat that at least three times a day." I sheepishly agreed to do it, not believing that repeating a phrase would have any power over the extreme of my anger and hurt. But whether it was from embarrassment over my small-mindedness in her company, or the efficacy of her remedy, I have to say it slowly opened my heart. In many ways she embodied the largess of love and she taught it to all of us just by her presence. One of the last lines in the show was hers: "There are many chambers in my heart." Again, a lesson I will keep close.

Sexual Abuse

Working on *Growing up Female* was the first time I realized the magnitude of the problem of sexual abuse. Once the first story of it came out in our group, the doors opened, and the women felt the permission and support to share their own often shameful and horrific stories. It was like a dam had broken and our rehearsals became a safe haven for unshed tears, dark memories, and a floodgate of emotion. I remember being shocked at the high percentage of the women in the group who had experienced sexual abuse, and it was then I realized how pervasive, and often hidden, it is in our society. I decided we had to create a scene about it and that it needed to be a collective story. The scene was shared onstage by four of the women who'd experienced sexual abuse, with each of them speaking lines and words in an overlapping fashion.

> …You were our bosses, our brothers, our fathers, our friends, our priests, our babysitters, our uncles, our grandfathers, our dates, our doctors, our cousins…
> All people who we trusted, or *thought* we could trust.
> My love became promiscuous.
> My love became non-existent. I froze up.
> I stopped eating. I tried to disappear.
> I *started* eating so I could hide in fat.
> For a long time my mind forgot—but my body remembered.
> I had nightmares.
> Night terrors.
> I took a lot of baths.
> I left my body.
> I lost my body.
> I lost myself.

I knew that to conclude this part with the women expressing feelings of "being lost" to themselves was too disempowering. I needed to find some "medicine" in this story. I can no longer remember exactly how the initial idea came up for the following section, but I do remember sitting in a circle on the floor with the women contributing ideas:

> We hereby declare the Women's Bill of Rights
> We have the right to *be* safe and to *feel* safe.
> We have the right to break the silence.
> We have the right to say no.
> We have the right to have loving intimate relationships.
> We have the right to wear what we want to wear.
> We have the right to walk where we want
> and work where we want.
> We have the right to exist.
> We have the right to be heard.

We have the right to heal.
We have the right to claim our sexuality.
We have the right not just to survive—but to thrive and grow.
We Hereby *Demand*
That everyone takes responsibility
To make sure that this never happens
To any girl or woman again.

There was strength and solidarity in this declaration, and women in the audience responded vociferously. That was the medicine.

A Woman's Strength

Strength is the first word that comes to mind when I think of Hilda. When we began working together in *Growing up Female*, Hilda was by her own description an angry black woman who'd been deeply wounded by racism, sexism, and poverty. But that description does no justice to the loving, wise, strong woman of great faith who became one of the most central performers in our group. Hilda cried her way through many rehearsals. She shouted with anger and she laughed loudly and often. Her story was screaming to be heard.

One day I asked the group to sit in a circle, rub their hands together, and then observe them. Then, while they kept their gaze on their own hands, I gave them the instructions to go one by one around the circle, saying out loud "These hands…" and fill in the blank. We went around the circle many times without time to think or censor, and the responses were amazing. It became clear that people could say things about themselves they might not usually disclose, but when it's about their hands, the words come flowing out: "These hands rocked my babies, these hands held my mother's hand while she was dying, these hands hammer, these hands are getting old, these hands have fought…" are just a few of the examples. I now use this exercise in almost all groups I lead and am always moved by it. I remember being particularly moved by Hilda's responses and decided to have her do her part sitting on a chair speaking, making hand gestures as she spoke:

These hands
These women's hands,
Have cooked, combed hair, sewed, needle pointed,
soothed my children,
And picked tobacco, down south in Georgia
while at my Grandmother's house.
Five dollars a day, thirty-five dollars a week.

These hands made drapes,
Beautiful long flowing drapes.
To hide the walls—the concrete walls of the projects
where I lived as a child
And then again as a woman.

These hands
These tough, calloused hands don't give up.
My father told me that the only reason I try so hard is because
someone told me that I couldn't.
He was right.
These hands don't accept no for an answer.

These hands
These women's hands
Hammer, cut, build, fabricate,
Pour 500 yards of concrete and drive forklifts and dump trucks.
These hands do not want to be told "Hilda, go get the coffee."

These hands were the first women's hands to become members of
Carpenter Local 626.
These hands were not always welcomed there—because these are
women's hands.
So when these hands,
Were down in the ditch for over 13 weeks, working,
trying to finish the last two weeks of apprenticeship,
And the boss came down,
These hands did not want to hear crude sexual remarks.

These hands got angry.
They remembered the strength that they felt in the hands of
Rosa Parks
And pulled my body out of the hole, up that ladder, grabbed that
boss and spun him around.

And after the boss said "You're fired,"
These hands were so grateful for the comradery and friendship of
co-workers Buddy Harris, Bob Anderson, and Nat Dunphy.
These male friends stood up for me and made sure that
justice was done.

These hands,
These proud hands, were with me when I walked across the stage
in November 1982
The night of my son's birthday
To a standing ovation
To receive my journeyman's certificate.

These hands are women's hands
Proud women's hands
Strong women's hands
Praying women's hands
My hands.

I don't think any of us were prepared for the cheering mid-show that followed Hilda's part. It gave her tremendous confidence and opened up a new path for her. Hilda eventually left her job as a carpenter and became a minister in the United Methodist Church. She claims it all began with *Growing up Female* and, if it hadn't been for the experience of sharing her story onstage, she might still be stuck in her anger and hurt.

Blessings from Kate

When Kate performed with us in *Growing up Female* at age 91, she was like a beacon of love. I became interested in how that could be passed on. Could we design a scene that modeled these connections she had made with all of us? One of the ways I decided to do it was to have the women and girls give blessings to each other and pass on their wisdom. The section ended with Kate, and I can still picture her beaming as she looked slowly out over all the women and girls onstage:

> Blessings. On each of you.
> And courage to risk mistakes.
> Make the most of wherever you are.
> Keep growing and live a full life.

It wasn't just her words. It was the 91 years of living and loving that were their foundation.

Growing up Female was Kate's third Theatre of Witness production. She was a great cheerleader for the process. She loved being part of the productions and believed in the power of the work. I remember earlier when we were making a film version of *Years* and, as is customary with filming, it was a long day with many starts and stops. I was worried about Kate's stamina and apologized for the long intervals with nothing to do. She looked at me with total amazement, and she said something I'll never forget: "It's not often we get called upon to give our all. Especially older people. I'm having a wonderful time." By the time we got to *Growing up Female* I trusted her great spirit and fortitude. Even as death approached, she was indomitable.

Towards the end of our tour of performances, Kate fell ill. She missed one rehearsal for an upcoming show, but wanted to come to the next one. Afterwards she wrote me a note saying that being with the group had been the medicine she needed and she felt much better. She performed in the last show we performed. And then she was diagnosed with cancer and died a brief time later. But Kate didn't go quietly. Before her death, she invited us to a tea party at her house so she could be with the women who'd been in the tea party scene with her. We filmed her beaming at everyone as she said her goodbyes not just to all of us, but also to life itself: "I'm dying in God's peace. Do not fear death, for you never meet. For where death is, you are not. Where you are, death is not. You never meet." The women all talked of death and said their goodbyes to a joyful Kate who was looking forward to this next chapter. Just about a week before she died, she called me and asked if we could videotape her. When we came to her home, she was propped up in her bed, almost ecstatic with excitement. She kept talking about how beautiful the dying process was and how there was nothing to fear. "I am having the most beautiful death anyone could imagine."

Kate never stopped teaching, she never stopped loving, and her spirit has never been separate from me. When I get stuck in the work or in my personal life, I hear her voice in my head urging me on, ever positive, always having faith in the process and in me. Knowing her has been one of the biggest blessings of my life.

CHAPTER 6

Living with Life

Prisoners

PHOTO © PATENTED PHOTOS

Only one minute in time has passed,
and yet all has forever changed.

From *Living with Life*

The morning of September 11, 2001 I was driving to a state
correctional institution in Chester, Pennsylvania when I heard on
the radio that the twin towers had just fallen. Like most of us
that day, I had no idea how to interpret what was happening,

what to do, or where to go next. I thought about going home, but something propelled me onwards towards the prison where I had an appointment to meet 16 lifers about a Theatre of Witness project I'd been invited in to propose to them. It was to be about what it means to serve a life sentence.

My decision to go on to my meeting was based on the belief that the incarcerated men would understand about catastrophe and trauma, and that the prison would probably be safe from outside terrorism. Mostly, though, I'd always felt a great calling to work with prisoners. I'm not sure why, but ever since I'd been young, I felt some affinity for those who were behind bars, and I wanted to know more about their lives and dreams. I assumed that they had wrestled with the biggest of life's issues and I felt I'd have so much to learn from them. I'd tried in vain to be invited in during the past ten years, and I didn't want to give up this opportunity. What I didn't expect was that being with the men would feel deeply comforting, real, and holy. It was the first of many moments in my time with them that would change all of our lives.

When I arrived, the men were sitting around a large conference table with the superintendent, the deputy, and the program manager. They reported that it was the first time the lifers had ever had permission to meet together as a group. Following the meeting, there was going to be a memorial service in the chapel to honor those killed by the terrorist attacks. The air was somber but charged. We all knew that something momentous was unfolding in the larger society, but were grateful for the focus that this meeting afforded us. The lifers introduced themselves and said a few words about their interest in the project. But before they went any further, they wanted to hear from me and see whether I could be trusted with their stories.

I began by talking about Theatre of Witness and I showed them video excerpts of works I'd created with refugees, women living in poverty, and survivors and perpetrators of abuse and violence. The men seemed moved by the stories of the performers on video. I could feel the emotion, concentration, and energy in the room. It was palpable.

Some of the men asked tough questions. Who would write the show? (I would, based on the words and stories of the men gleaned in interviews and rehearsals. They'd have total veto power over every word.) Would anyone make money off of it? (No, I was working through my non-profit company TOVA and we were using grant money to fund the project. In fact, lack of funds was a constant struggle.) What were the themes going to be? (I had no idea. These would come from the men directly.) There was also a lot of excitement and creative energy expressed. In the end, eight men said that they wanted to participate and commit to coming to two or three meetings a week for up to six months. We were extremely lucky that all of the eight had wonderful stage presence, stories, and musical ability.

This project was an opportunity to delve deeply into what it means to live with a life sentence in a state where there is no possibility of parole. Our intention was to share these stories with the prison population, as well as the general public, to help people understand the inner lives of prisoners. I don't think any of us had any clue as to how big this project would become, or that it would eventually be seen and lauded by prisoners and staff, judges, legislators, victim groups, families of prisoners, criminologists, and activists. We all entered into the project as if it was an important soul journey we each had to make. A journey we each took individually, as well as in the company of each other.

At the initial meeting, the one caveat given to me by the superintendent was that the show needed to be titled *Living with Life*, a concept that had been in her heart for a long time. Looking back now, I see how particular and open-ended that title was. It gave the audience a chance to peer into the lives of prisoners and ask how lifers live with their sentence. But it also invited us all to examine our own lives and ask ourselves, how do we live a life? Other than the instruction for the title of the project, I was given fairly free rein. In fact, it was only a few days before the first public show that anyone from the administration asked to see a rehearsal or script. I know enough now to be very grateful for this almost unprecedented freedom.

From the beginning, I was deeply curious about the lives of these men. I wanted to understand what it was like to know that you were going to spend the rest of your life in prison, knowing that you'd never again see the night sky, trees, your home, or possibly even some of your family members. I wondered how one lives with the guilt, shame, and/or horror of knowing that your actions resulted in the taking of a life. I wondered how the men who got a mandatory life sentence for second-degree murder dealt with the inhumanity of the sentence. (Some of the men I worked with had been look-outs on robberies that turned into homicides. They themselves hadn't been where the shooting happened and, in some cases, didn't even hold guns.) I wondered about those who proclaimed their innocence.

I knew that these men who had spent more than 177 cumulative years in prison, some of them in solitary confinement, many of them in fear, isolation, and loneliness, were experts at deep reflection. I saw that I, who paid money to take refuge in monastic meditation settings with great masters, might learn more from prisoners, who also were living a life of renunciation, than from teachers who were willingly embracing lives of simplicity. These men had lost their identities, families, occupations, and freedom. They'd eaten, swallowed, and digested questions that some of us barely take the time to acknowledge. They'd looked their demons in the eye and had found ways to live with what many of us would find unbearable. They would become my teachers.

While I knew that our mutual exploration would teach me plenty, I was also cognizant that questions about love, belonging, forgiveness, and service resonate differently for those who are imprisoned and those who are free. Asking to whom one belongs is different when you and your loved ones are separated by a prison wall and the only shared time you can ever have together is in a crowded prison visiting room. The question of whether one's sins are forgiven feels different when the person asking is serving time for murder. By my asking these questions, the performers had a chance to speak out loud about things they'd never shared. They were giving voice to that which had remained voiceless.

From the very beginning I loved being with the men. They were extremely open and there was a real intimacy in our connection. I found in my time with them, and later in subsequent prison projects, that being in a penitentiary can feel like being held in a laser beam. There's a concentration of intense energy and focus that lends itself to depth and honesty. I learned so much about gratitude, being in the moment, and yes, even joy, while being there. I was extremely lucky—in all five prison projects, I got to work with the *crème de la crème*—men who had already done deep reflection and inner change work. They were trustworthy, serious, and deep. They were also so appreciative of the opportunity being afforded them to tell their stories, that they didn't waste a moment. In fact, they worked harder than any group I've ever worked with. Sometimes I'd come into the prison for rehearsal, and even though I was on time, the men would already be assembled and directing themselves in a scene. This self-direction was unheard of in this work, and I've never experienced it before or since. I was able to bring my best to them, and they to me.

Wrestling with Atonement

Don was perhaps the most overtly tough of all the men, a very unlikely participant. He was a large white man who spoke with a thick Philadelphia accent. He reminded me of a heavy-set gangster from the Italian mafia, yet I could also see that under his gruff, "no-nonsense" persona was a genuine man, eager to try something new and challenging.

Don had been raised Catholic in a two-parent family in a row house in South Philadelphia where everyone looked out for one another. He'd had what he called a normal childhood, going to parochial school, working, getting married, having a child. But somewhere along the way, the streets and methamphetamines called to him and he succumbed to that state of fast-paced greed. He eventually became quite a hardened hustler and drug dealer. He told me that if I'd known him on the outside, I wouldn't have liked him—that he hadn't been a good person. Everything for him was very black-and-white. You were either a friend or an enemy.

When I'd asked him about what happened the night of the crime that had brought him to prison, he spoke about being in his warehouse, and another guy entering, ready to kill him. He indicated that some things aren't really a choice and that he did what he had to do in order to stay alive.

Don's religious faith was still very important to him and he went to Mass whenever it was offered. He often sought spiritual counseling and wrestled with issues of sin and forgiveness. Don spoke about the one question that perhaps tormented him more than any other when he asked whether the time he was serving was making up for the sins he'd committed. He wondered whether he'd go to heaven. For Don, heaven was the place where his mother, who'd passed away during his incarceration, now lived. This question became the "gold" for me, the hook that I used to script his part. I no longer remember if it was Don, the other men, the composer, or me who came up with the idea of using the melody of "Stairway to Heaven" as a background for his part. The men wrote new words and, much like a Greek chorus, sang behind him. In between verses, as they hummed harmonies, Don spoke his story:

> 1978. I was living the American dream
> I had a wife, a house, cars,
> A kid on the way
> But it wasn't enough. I wanted more.
> More money, more drugs, more action
> Something inside of me kept pulling me back to the streets
> I was out all night—hustling—working 14 hours at a clip
> Life was too fast, too easy and too dangerous
> Until that fateful night when we settled scores.
> Two people ended up dead on the floor
> And I was arrested
> Sitting in the courtroom, convicted of first degree murder
> Hearing the jury say LIFE without parole.
> It nearly tore me apart
> My lawyer said I'd be out in 20 years

> However, I found out that in Pennsylvania
> you never get out on a life sentence
> Life means just that…LIFE
> Now I lay here in my cell, thinking about it everyday
> Wondering if I'll ever get to go home…
>
> And I ask myself—will I go to heaven?

There was something startlingly real and direct about the way Don asked that last question. I always sensed that he really didn't know whether there was anything he could ever do here on earth that would atone for the great sin of murder. For him, heaven was real and he honestly didn't know whether he was eligible for entry. That burning question, emanating from a man with such a hardened exterior, always cut right through me. I think it affected the audience deeply as well.

It Was Me Who Did It

Shots (the street name given to him, reflecting his skill on the basketball court) was the performer who was most open about sharing the nature of his crime and what brought him to the penitentiary. A small black man with a deep-throated laugh and infectious smile, he was a fantastic singer and composer. Shots was also a deeply religious man who led the church choir. Being a peer leader in the prison who had successfully completed addiction treatment, he was quite used to sharing his story with others. However, I think that the creative process that we engaged in while developing *Living with Life* was something new for him, particularly the one-on-one deep-hearted listening interviews.

There was an intimacy that got fostered quite quickly in those initial interviews that allowed the men to talk about what was most on their hearts and minds. For some of them like Shots, our interviews became a chance to do a life review. He wanted to explore the trajectory that brought him to that fateful night:

> I was a bad boy. A bad, little boy. I bullied my brothers around. When I was 11 years old my mom and father were struggling. I felt they shouldn't be. So I stole. I stole for

the family. Stole money and bought food and put it in the refrigerator. Holidays I did the same thing. I'd steal money for gifts. I had a friend named Charley and he had a truck. I'd say: "Will you take these toys to my house?" We'd put them in the cellar for Christmas Eve. The next morning everyone had gifts... Then I began graduating in crime.

He spoke about burglaries and drug use, including the night when he swallowed 13 Valium and fell asleep in his bed. He was awakened by a group of his friends who reminded him that he'd agreed to be the lookout during a robbery they had planned for later that night in a bar. Shots protested to them that he was ready to turn his life around, but they reminded him that he had given his word that he'd hold the guns one more time:

> The bar was around the corner. Everyone knew us. I was so out of it that I walked down the streets with the guns in my hand. They had to tell me to put them away. They announced a hold-up and herded everyone into the pool-room. I watched as they lined everyone up against the wall and began patting them down. I had the guns down by my side, but I blanked out and went into a nod. The next thing I heard was someone screaming "Stop! Don't move!" I woke up and startled as I raised the guns. I must have accidentally pulled the trigger. The shot went off. I looked around to see if the blast hit anyone. I saw my friends run out. I stepped to the side and saw a guy lying there in a pool of blood on the floor. All the people in the bar were looking at me. I looked at everyone. I looked down on the floor. The guy lying there was my cousin William Boyd. I killed him.

Told onstage with background music and lighting, Shots always dramatized this scene in the most realistic yet poetic way. He relived each moment in slow motion, revealing layers of emotion and sensations that left no doubt that this was his own life story, however painful it was. We always saw his shocked and horrified reaction to the realization that he'd taken someone's life, and that there was absolutely nothing he could do now to change it. It was clear that he put himself through this, night after night onstage, for the purpose of helping the audience understand how drugs, the street life, and criminal activity often escalate into a tragedy with consequences too terrible to bear.

Although Shots had essentially told this story in his own words many times before in the context of group meetings within the prison, I think the fullness of performing it with all the artistic elements of music, lighting, and other performers added a dimension that also brought him to new depths. It gave him an opportunity to publicly claim responsibility and express his remorse. A remorse that he had privately expressed in tears during one of our interviews:

> I apologize to my family and I apologize to my son. I wasn't there for him. I apologize to the victim's family. I wonder who my victim would have been. Maybe a mechanic. Maybe a movie star. I don't know. I took that right from him. I apologize to anybody whom my crime may have affected. If my victim could live these next 27 years and I could take his place, I would. I really mean that from the bottom of my heart. 'Cause I lived a good life.

At this point, Shots looked out towards the audience. His demeanor softened as he got more personal:

> Is my mother out there?
> I apologize to you Ma for taking you through all these troubles for all these years.
> I'm sorry.

The apology onstage gave Shots an opportunity to deeply communicate with his family and it always brought me to tears. I'd met his mother, father, and brother in their home a few months previously, when he, like a few of the men, had suggested I meet some of their family members. I was more than happy to be a bridge between them and the prison, something not usually afforded staff or volunteers. I will always remember the first time that I went to Shots' childhood home in the inner city. His mother, father, and I sat together in the small but comfortable living room. Shots had just written a new song that we'd recorded for rehearsal, and when I realized that I had a copy with me on CD, I offered to play it for his parents.

[*Chorus:*]
Another night.
While I'm lying here alone
In my bed so cold,
Not as warm as yesterday
But in my mind, I'm thinking of how things used to be
It seems so real, how did it slip away, from me?

[*Voiceover:*]
Attention all areas, attention all areas! 2,100 count is commencing.
2,100 count is commencing. Lights on, two officers at your door.

If we could only change back the hands of time
Do things different than we do today
Amazing how a few minutes can change a life
How a few moments can change so many people's lives
The older you get, the more wise you become
You see mistakes
How can I ask for forgiveness
When because of me, another's life was robbed?
How do I make amends?
When I think of the lives I've affected—
not just the life of the victim, it's hard.
It's very hard.
Just like I want to live—they wanted to live
But I can't turn back the hands of time.

There is no way to describe the multitude of emotions that we all felt when we heard him sing about being all alone in his cell at night, as his beautiful singing voice flooded the living room; a room he hadn't been in for 28 years. As I sat on the worn sofa, looking across at his mother and father, I realized that this was the first time they'd heard Shots sing since his incarceration more than 20 years earlier. For one moment in time, he was back at home with his family, pouring his heart out through music. And I was so grateful for the opportunity to bridge the prison walls.

Of all the music that Shots helped to write, I think the song "Hold On" was the one that hit the very essence of what it means to serve a life sentence. During my private interviews with the men, they all spoke about the fear that one day they would go insane from the confinement of being behind bars for life. They also shared that it wasn't anything they ever spoke about with each other. One day in rehearsal I said, "I've heard you all talk individually about your fear of going insane in prison—let's talk about it together." I then directed them all to speak and improvise simultaneously to illustrate what the experience of going crazy felt like.

Very quickly, it became terrifyingly real. As they physicalized their distress, they paced, rocked, sweat, and shook, and I felt the anxiety level in the room rise precipitously. Wanting to shift the energy, I asked them how they coped with the flood of feeling when they feared that they were losing their minds. "What do you hold on to?" That's when, together, they came up with a soothing melody and began to improvise lyrics that displayed the range of survival skills they used to calm themselves. Singing was the primary one for Shots:

> Hold on to memories
> See what tomorrow brings
> Hold on to family
> Hold on to dignity
> Hold on to me
> Hold on
>
> Hold on to sanity
> It's been a mystery
> Forget about yesterday
> My mind is here to stay
> At night I pray
> Hold on

> Death Row. I wake up every night screaming. Hollering. Tears in my eyes. I hear hollering and the guys say it's me. It feels like 25 thousand volts running through my body. In daytime you wouldn't know anything is wrong. But my hair is falling out and I got ulcers. At night when my mind is at ease, the madness makes me scream. I'm screaming in my sleep.

> Over the years, I've seen men try all kinds of things to cope with prison life.

I've seen people stabbed, cut their wrists, hang it up. I've seen men turn into mice, them turn to other men, go to mental hospitals or become so institutionalized that they no longer care about anything.

When you stop holding on, it's over…

The staging for this song, with the men gently leaning on each other, was for me the most moving part of the show. There was something so surprising about seeing male prisoners unabashedly hold onto each other in their sorrow and vulnerability. It's something that I never would have dared to impose, knowing that it would seem hokey or unreal. But it evolved naturally as the men reached out for each other as they became more open with themselves, the process, and each other. It was the part of the show and subsequent film that almost always reduced me to tears.

Following the end of our performances, I interviewed each man individually as part of closure. The time I spent with Shots was one of the deepest and most intimate I've ever spent with anyone. We sat across from each other in an empty room and Shots wept his heart out. His tears drew my own out, as I felt his deep sorrow. It was one of those moments that I know will be with me on my deathbed, a moment of such stark truth, pain, and connection. There was nothing for me to do, no physical connection with him to make. It was just two people in a room together, one feeling the other's deepest pain with no barriers to full vulnerability. I am beyond grateful for his trust in me and for the beauty of that time together.

Still Standing

Al's part was about transformation, love, and dignity, qualities many of us might think are rare in prison—but they're not.

With the beginnings of gray hair, wireless glasses, and a calm and wise presence, Al was the "old head" of our group. Soft spoken with an almost Southern lilt to his voice, he carried himself with a straight-backed dignity. But back in the Sixties, he'd been part of the Black Panther movement and had been considered a revolutionary. During those turbulent times, a police officer and park guard were killed in Philadelphia, and Al was charged with conspiracy, treated as "public enemy number one," and given a life sentence.

But the Al I knew was shy, gentle, and deeply introspective. He often spoke about love and spirituality:

> Love is like a cloud moving so gracefully. You can see it in a look, a touch, a smile… Spirituality is a lifelong thing that you can never get enough of. It's unlimited. Ever-present. Not only in humans, but in all living things.

Al told me about his ability to go deep within himself and intervene in any dis-ease of his body. He was able to actually visualize his internal organs and then redirect his energy towards healing. His soft presence seemed to me to be in direct contradiction to the "cop killer" image the media had painted of him during his multiple trials. I wanted the audience to "rehumanize" him too.

For a long while, I didn't have a "hook" for his part, and saved scripting it until more than a month after I'd finished everyone else's parts. It was only when I turned his phrase "I remain still standing" over and over in my mind that I realized that it was the "gold" in his story.

> In 1997—after 27 years of incarceration, they called me down and said that if I testified against my co-defendant, they'd do everything in their power to release me. I grew up with certain values and I had a certain reputation of being honest, upright and dependable in prison. After 27 years, witnesses were dead. They were asking me to lie. They wanted me to testify that I saw him pull the trigger. Even if I had seen it, I wouldn't have testified. Prison is a city within a city. Being a snitch is a cruel life in prison. I lost a lot by not testifying. I lost my freedom. I lost my family. But what I didn't lose was my dignity, my self-respect. Me.

Whenever Al spoke those words, he stood straight-backed, facing the audience with a sense of quiet dignity. The impact of his having served more than 32 years behind bars at that point was palpable. For me, that amount of time seemed endless, yet Al's spirit was unbroken. I began to imagine him standing at the window bars, looking out as 32 winters turn into springs, silently witnessing and even appreciating the passage of time.

> Seasons change
> Prisoners come and go
> Lifers grow older and some die never leaving this place
> Hearts beat, blood flows
> Wars begin, families disintegrate
> New men enter the system and new leaders fight for justice
> Children and grandchildren are born and grow
> Some meet their fathers for the first time in prison
> Leaves fall, colors change
> I watch it all from behind these walls

The composer and I then put his words to song. I asked the men to slowly walk around him as Al stood still, looking carefully at each man as they passed in front of him. The men all sang the chorus together:

> I've seen seasons change
> Blood flows in my veins
> And I, I remain still standing
>
> I've seen spring and fall
> Behind prison walls
> And I, I remain still standing
>
> I've seen the face of war and hate
> I've heard the call of reason
> I've seen the power of love on earth
>
> And I believe in healing…
>
> I've seen seasons change
> Blood flows in my veins
> And I, I remain still standing

Music and lyrics by Greg Scott

Over the years, when I screen the video of the production for a group, I always close with Al's part. I then ask participants to stand up when they feel ready and answer one of the following questions out loud: "What do you stand for? On whose shoulders are you standing? With whom do you stand?" When everyone is up and has spoken, we make a circle, look around the room, and remark on the good company we keep. I like to think that Al's wisdom, even behind bars, has the power to make strangers reflect on their own life stance.

Ripples of Change

Something changed in the prison for a while. For a period of time, a moment in our collective history together, an energy of possibility took over. Within the prison, there was a flurry of excitement; certain trusted correctional officers helped the men learn their lines; building staff constructed the stage in the chapel; counselors met together; and the administration sent out invitations to VIPs. Fellow prisoners as well as staff broke open with emotion during performances. Many rocked in their seats, openly wept, and hugged each other. They stood in ovations. They expressed gratitude. For those six to twelve months, the cast members became heroes. Staff looked at them differently, many of them seeing for the first time the man inside the uniform: the father, son, husband, friend. Correctional officers and staff wrote letters thanking us. They invited their own families to come and witness the show. They wrote recommendations. Many staff as well as fellow prisoners began to ask them for advice. A common humanity was exposed.

And the experience of witnessing the performances in the prison transformed audience members, many of who—had never been in a prison before. For them, the experience surrounded them from the moment they were first escorted through the corridors, doors locking behind them. Seeing prisoners out in the yard, looking at them through the windows, became, for many, a confrontation with the reality of racism and imprisonment that left them frightened, outraged, and overwhelmed. As they sat in the chapel, waiting for the performance to begin, many felt trapped and enclosed, furthering the impact of the experience. Once the performance began, there was no doubt that these were real lifers in a real prison, talking, singing, and crying about the impact that their crimes and imprisonment had had on their own lives, as well as those of their victims and families. When the cast members reached the final scenes in which they apologized and sang "Hold on to me," each performance became a communal catharsis.

The family members of the performers who were present in the audience also added to the emotional tone of the experience. One performer looked out one night, and delivered his apology right to his mother with tears in his eyes: "Mama, you've gone through so much. Please forgive me. I love you girl." And yet, it was just as profound when their families were absent. Al looked out to the audience one night and spoke his words directly to them:

> Early in my sentence I was bitter. I couldn't see my life being cut off at such a young age—25. In 1970 I was a husband with two sons and a daughter who I haven't seen since. If two of my children were sitting out here with you all tonight, I wouldn't recognize them. But after a while you realize that you can't stay bitter, you still have to grow. In prison you see people who never knew how to read or write. You can be helpful here too. Your bitterness is not as important.

At each performance the chaplain led everyone in prayer, and audience members were given the opportunity to ask questions and give testimony. One woman from a victim's group said, "I didn't want to ever hear the stories of prisoners. My brother was murdered on the streets and I have had no feelings of compassion towards the man who murdered him. But since hearing you all, for the first time, I can say that my heart is open. Thank you." We also heard from family members of some of the performers. The grown son of one of the men stood up and said, "That's my father up there. I never knew what you did. I never knew your story. Tonight, I want to pledge to you all that I will not follow in your footsteps, but instead will stay out of the street life. Dad—I love you." That's when I realized that this whole project was much bigger than the production of a play in prison. The ritual of theatre was serving as a communal catharsis, bringing prisoners and those who loved, knew, or feared them together to grieve and heal. *Living with Life* gave all of us a chance to shift the perspective so together we could witness the effects that incarceration has on the soul of a society.

None of us were prepared for the outpouring of feeling in the audiences, the desire that many felt to rush towards the men with hugs and tears, totally surrounding them. It was often overwhelming to the men, who weren't used to being touched. Years in prison had taught them to grow internal body armor that protected their personal space. But quickly, they adapted, overwhelmed by the flood of support and love.

After these public performances, audiences asked how they could become advocates for change in Pennsylvania's arcane criminal justice laws. They spoke about the need for the show to be seen around the world. They wanted to spread the word. And with all of that, the men began to believe that change might actually happen. They believed that there was the energy and will to change laws. They believed that it was worth investing in the hope that their sentences might be commuted, and/or that Pennsylvania would change its mandatory life sentence law for second degree murder. They believed that something profound had happened and "all would forever change." I wonder about the efficacy of those expectations, though. Theatre director Erik Ehn has asked why we evaluate theatre by whether it's effected change in politics, and yet we don't evaluate politics by whether it has changed art. I think it's an important question. In the ten years since the production, the state of Pennsylvania has not repealed its sentencing laws and the prison offers fewer opportunities for inmate education and expression. Seven of the eight performers are still behind bars, and there are 3500 lifers incarcerated in Pennsylvania alone. Yet, miraculously, this past year, one of the men had his life sentence commuted by the governor, and after 36 years of incarceration, he is out on parole.

I now think back to a pivotal discussion I had with the mother of one of the cast members. She was a frail woman who had endured the murder of one of her sons and the life sentence of the other. She once whispered to me that she knew that her faith was strong enough to set her son free. But she was afraid that he himself didn't have the same faith. So she believed it was her job to help him see that if both of them prayed together with the same absolute conviction and belief, the prison gates would one day open and he would walk home, a free man. When I felt the strength of her faith, I asked myself whether perhaps faith really could become contagious. And maybe that is what is fair to ask of Theatre of Witness—that the vehicle of story and testimony opens minds and hearts, passes on the positive qualities of love, forgiveness, redemption, and transformation, and in that, becomes a seed for change. That is more than enough for me.[1]

---

1 Adapted from "Living with Life: The Theatre of Witness as a Model of Healing and Redemption." In Jonathan Shailor (2010) *Performing New Lives: Prison Theatre.* London and Philadelphia: Jessica Kingsley Publishers. Reproduced with permission of Jessica Kingsley Publishers.

CHAPTER 7

Standing at the Doorway

Runaway Girls in Poland

PHOTO © LUKASZ TURA

In 2003 I was invited by the director of the Silesian Dance Company to create a Theatre of Witness production with runaway teenage girls in Bytom, Poland. When I realized that the school that housed the girls was close to where my grandmother Tessa emigrated from, there was no way I could refuse.

Before my trip, I dreamed that I was walking through a landscape of hands that were growing up from under the ground. Fingers were reaching, stretching, and grabbing at my feet and legs from underneath the earth. At first I was petrified that they were trying to pull me under to share in their death. But then I realized that the hands only wanted to touch me. To touch a Jew who had returned—alive. The thought came that we weren't all exterminated. Some of us returned.

Erasure

The project began with me studying Polish for a month in the city of Lublin, a city that had once been the center of a vibrant Jewish community and home to some of the most famous mystic rebbes.[1] But in 2003 our absence was palpable. The death camp at Majdanek, a few miles down the road, no longer sent up plumes of smoke, but there were less than 20 Jews left in Lublin. In our history class we read newspapers from the 1930s and 1940s, which talked of "exterminating Jewish vermin." This historic anti-Semitism got to me, and for the first time in my life I was aware of my own deep, internalized oppression. I felt invisible.

I was terrible at learning Polish, by far the slowest in my class. Appalled at how little I could communicate, I felt humiliated and vulnerable, often leaving the class at breaks to cry in the ladies' room. Each day I sat behind a desk in class, watching the teacher at the blackboard write out conjugations and vocabulary words. She wrote and erased, wrote and erased. Not understanding or remembering what things meant, I had trouble concentrating, and became intrigued with the eraser—the rubbing out of words, ideas, connections. With each erasure of a word, I felt as though I too was being blotted out. In Poland, my people no longer existed. In Poland, I no longer existed. I was stripped of my identity as a mother, daughter, artist. I felt like a young child trying to decipher the world around me, but my adult-size ego was crushed by its invisibility.

I realized that in some small way this must be how the refugees I worked with felt when they landed in a new country, unable to speak. Unlike them, I had food, shelter, and work at the profession I loved, but still, I felt annihilated. Later, when working

---

1 "Rebbe" is Yiddish for "rabbi."

with the runaway girls, I recognized a similar sense of invisibility, insecurity, and silence. I had unknowingly taken a small step into their inner world.

Running

On the train to Bytom to meet the girls for the first time, I was immediately struck by the endless gray and brown of the land. Bytom is a former coal mining area, with a lot of poverty. The polluted air was dark, textured, and rough. It was a dark that muted all colors and seeped into my bones. At night, the few streetlights cast a yellowish haze in circles of fog. I was scared to walk alone. Sometimes I opened my mouth just to drink in the darkness. I wondered if I could breathe it in fully, savoring each molecule.

Each day I walked a shortcut that took me between the Catholic cemetery on my right, ablaze with candles and brightly colored flowers sitting on top of each grave, and the brown, empty playground to my left. It was a noiseless place with worn-out dirt and a lone, stilled swing set. The silence confused me as I walked between the dead and the not yet dead. It was all mixed up there, the living and the not.

The girls I worked with in the school were fragile and haunted. They lived in this small residential school as a last resort after years of anti-social behavior, playing hooky, or having no safe family with whom to live. Most had been so abused and abandoned that sometimes it was almost too painful to look into their eyes.

A person cannot forget such things

She threw me out

She gave me away

A rope around his neck

I saw it all

I brought two translators with me to the school, both gentle and caring souls. They, too, were moved by the vulnerability of the girls, and I often saw tears in their eyes. We'd all sit across from each other in the day room, a cold, concrete block of a room, cluttered with posters and pictures of the girls. We could hear students running and yelling down the halls outside the door. The process of speaking and listening was slow. When we met as a full group in a circle on the gym floor, Natalia whispered the girls' Polish words into English, directly into my ear, while Tomek became my Polish voice. Conversation took twice as long while they translated every word between us. It meant that there were long periods of listening when the girls and I just looked at each other. The waiting and watching took on its own slow, rhythmic dance. I was mesmerized by their eyes. All that I saw was the suffering they had endured. Their stories came out in bits and pieces:

She told me she hated me. "I'm not your mother anymore."

He took a knife and he tried to kill me

I was only seven

I had bruises all over my body

She left for two years

I could do nothing. I was standing. Completely still.

Time got slower. I did nothing. I couldn't say a word.

I cried inside of myself.

I ran away

I was always escaping

I was alone

Running

Away

The first girl I interviewed individually was Agata. A tall girl with light brown hair pulled back in a ponytail, she had learned a few words of English, and loved to say "hello," "goodbye," and "thank you" to me. In turn, I practiced my "*dziekuję*" (thank you), and we'd laugh at my paltry success. Agata was patient with me, and I think she liked being seen as someone who could help me in my struggle to learn this difficult language. I sensed a great strength in her from her smiling eyes. But when she spoke about her childhood, those very eyes clouded and dimmed. A hollow, vacant look descended:

> My youngest childhood I don't remember.
>
> But my brother and sister tell me that one day when I was an infant, I was crying. My father was drunk and wanted me to stop. So he took a knife and tried to kill me.
>
> My life later was almost the same.
>
> When I was seven, my parents started to drink
> and we had those quarrels.
> My father abused my older brother and me.
> He would be yelling and beating the hell out of us for small things.
> I cried. I was small.
> When I was nine or ten, my mother came home so drunk that she was vomiting and there was blood. I was sitting beside her and crying. I cried so badly 'cause I thought that she was dying.
>
> I ended up at an institution because I stopped going to school.
> The police found me, and when my parents came to the station to bring me home, I refused to go home with them.
> I'm not ashamed for being here or for what happened to me.
> It's not me who should be ashamed.
>
> Sometimes I go into my room and I am sad and don't feel like living anymore.
> In my heart is emptiness. It's gray.

One day early on in the interview process, I wanted to tap into Agata's inner strength. I led her in some guided imagery and asked her to imagine the animal she most identified with. She lit up: "I am a big black horse, running, running free in the field." Just saying those words brought a wide grin to her face. I kept that image at the forefront in my work with her, knowing that it was with this beautiful, strong horse that we would both ally.

When Polish teachers, social workers, and other artists asked about my project, many of them questioned whether the Theatre of Witness model could work in Poland. They wondered if it was an American form that suited our more open society. They had fears that the girls wouldn't open up, and that audiences wouldn't want to hear their stories of pain. But I trusted that the girls, just like people everywhere, would want to be known, heard, and accepted. I also had faith in the creative process and held a clear vision in my mind's eye of the girls performing and audiences drinking it in. Little did I know early on how strongly my faith would be tested.

Some late afternoons, when I arrived for rehearsal, one or two of the girls would still be lying in their beds in their dorm rooms with their blankets covering their faces. Some days all they wanted to do was cry. Other days they were eager and waiting for us to arrive. It was a rollercoaster, and I didn't know what was possible. I began to question whether they'd ever be strong enough to actually tell their stories onstage. Tomek, my translator, wrote a haiku one night for them: "Little gray bird, tell me about the sky." We waited, and coaxed, and listened. But after a few months I realized that the psychological effects of the traumas they'd suffered were still so present, that I couldn't imagine them being able to perform. I wasn't even sure it would be a good idea. Thoughts of defeat engulfed me and I thought maybe it would be better to cut our losses before the whole project imploded. But then I realized that if I went home, the girls would be left, living the legacy of one more failure. And as I pictured their pleading eyes and budding womanliness, I knew that I had to ally with their strength. I pictured Agata's black horse. There was no going home.

The Land That Was Once Home

Personally, at this point in the process, I wasn't even sure where my home was. I too was becoming dislocated. Being in Poland triggered ancient memories of pogroms, Jewish shtetl life, and the concentration camps, and I seemed to be living between worlds. I felt my ancestors' erasure. While participating in an intense five-day Bearing Witness retreat at the Auschwitz and Birkenau concentration camps, I found myself scouring the photo gallery at the museum about Jewish life before the war, looking for my own picture hanging on the wall. I was trying to find my father and me. It was only after peering into scores of faded black and white photos that I remembered that I was born in 1950 in the United States and had never lived in Poland. But this intellectual knowledge made no dent in my desperate attempt to retrieve myself. Maybe I looked different then, in the early twentieth century, before we all died. I was now a tourist in the land that was once home.

In Poland, Catholic graves are covered with flowers and candles in a riot of color that lights up the night sky. The dead are visited regularly by family members who decorate headstones with bouquets and wreaths. The cemeteries are filled with visitors, and are often the one spot of color in the endless gray and brown of the landscape.

The Old Jewish cemetery in Lublin is kept locked, surrounded by a thick black metal fence, and only one person has the key. The ground is littered with broken bottles and weeds. Trees grow through the graves of some of the most revered mystic rebbes. In the new Jewish cemetery, the dead also lay unattended. One day when I went there, a radio blared as a man repaired his motorcycle on the worn grass near the memorial building. Rubber and metal parts were strewn around him. Across the street, the Catholic cemetery was smothered with flowers.

After I described the Jewish cemetery to my Polish language teacher, she looked at me with great seriousness: "Don't the Jews care about their dead?"

Did this young Polish woman miss the Holocaust? Who did she think was left to tend to our graves? We are now only tourists in a land that was once home.

Step by Step

Back at the school, I'd watch Beata and Halinka snuggle inside the hoods of their sweatshirts, hiding, waiting, comforting themselves. Halinka was small and blonde with deep eyes, and a dimple when she smiled. She and Beata often clung to each other, resting their heads on each other's shoulders. Sometimes Halinka would peer out with big, vulnerable eyes, begging to be mothered. Could this young Polish Catholic girl and I become kin?

The girls' stories slowly emerged, but their capacity for this creative process was inconsistent. One day we couldn't get Maja to stop crying. Tomek sat with her on her bed for a few hours, strumming the guitar.

> The beatings from my father? I feel it still in my heart.
> My heart wanted to jump out.
> My heart was afraid that he'd do something to me and kill me.
> He always told me that he doesn't love me. He hates me...

> One day again, he came when my mother was out.
> He started beating me.
> I screamed I hate him, he should leave and he shouldn't
> enter our home when my mom was out.
> But what could I do—this vulnerable girl?
> I couldn't do anything. I'd get beaten more.

> So I stood still.
> I didn't breathe. I cried only on the inside.
> Time stopped as the bruises grew.
> My heart kept beating.
> I stood still.

It was clear that Maja was too vulnerable to perform, as were most of the girls. With much consternation, I finally conceded that we needed to move to Plan B. But I wanted to stay as true as I could to the central tenet of Theatre of Witness, of having people play their own life stories. So I came up with the solution that we'd have the girls onstage while young actresses played their parts. Hopefully there could be some minimal interaction between them. Maybe the girls would stand nearby, watching. Maybe they'd silently walk towards the front of the stage at the end, looking directly at the audience. Maybe this was the best we could do under the circumstances.

I had auditions and chose three beautiful young acting students from a nearby conservatory, each just a few years older than the girls. The actresses were scared, though, to meet the girls, and the day of their first visit, they cried on the bus going home. They were frightened of the girls' pain, and were afraid they wouldn't know how to hold their stories.

By this time I'd scripted the individual parts, and I asked the actresses to read them to themselves. I wanted them to be immersed in the girls' stories while we used our group rehearsal time to build community, performance skills, and trust. The actresses added energy and power when engaged in movement, games, and singing. They moved with authority and commitment that slowly began to inspire the girls to come out of their shells. Together, the actresses and I encouraged the girls to be silly, make mistakes, be bold and loud. We sat with them in a circle on the floor of the gym, listening quietly to the girls talk or cry. We breathed together. We hugged a lot, and we went slowly, step by step.

I Am Here But I Am Not

I fell in love with them—especially Halinka. We connected behind language, a trust that was palpable. Her story was deeply tragic, yet filled with poetic imagery. It was easy for me to find the gold in it—the metaphors and symbolism. One day I asked her to rehearse with the actress who was going to do her part. After Ewa performed it once, I asked Halinka, "How would you do it? Show us."

She stood up and moved with an authority and poetry I could never, ever have imagined. She knew every word, every place each gesture should occur. She was pure spirit.

> My childhood ended when I was six.
> I went to the playground and
> noticed a lot of people standing in front of my house.

> When I entered, I saw my father lying on the bathroom floor
> with a rope around his neck.
> I am at the doorway, I don't know whether to enter.

Halinka paused, her body becoming silent as she gazed at the imagined scene seared in her memory. Time stopped and then turned on itself. With just a slight tilt of her head and an upwards gaze, the doorway became visible to those of us watching. She stood at the threshold, poised but still. We imagined the scene through her eyes—her father's body in front of her on the floor. She then inhaled, turned to face us, and told us about playing hooky from school, living underground, and using drugs:

> I am afraid to go home.
> Sometimes my mother brings the food and money
> only to the front door.
> She won't let me in...

Halinka told of being put into an orphanage, hating it, and running away. Caught by the police, she was arrested, and at the station tried to cut her wrists. Finally she was brought to the reform school. It was her last chance. She wrote a poem about being locked in a golden cage flooded with tears, and we set the poem to music.

> I am here, but I am not
> The wind hears my cries
> The sun shines through the bars
> My sadness has a name
>
> Maybe you will give me your hand today
> To free me from that cage
> Maybe I'll fly like a free bird
> Maybe I'll sing to you about the sky
> Maybe I'll grow like a small flower
> On barren ground
>
> Someone is reaching for me.
> They open the door and hold out their hands.
> I stand at the doorway. I don't know whether I will enter.

Silent, with wide-open eyes, Halinka stood ready, and not knowing. When she finished, I looked at her: "Halinka, you know you have to perform this yourself. You are pure poetry." She nodded.

That night, the image of her standing at the doorway kept reverberating. I felt the anguish of this beautiful young woman, who was refused entry to her own home. I kept picturing her standing at the threshold—the threshold of womanhood, the threshold of danger, the threshold of possibility. What doors would open for her? Where would she be welcomed? Would she have the courage to step into a new life?

I went back to my flat and fingered my mezuzah, that lay wrapped in a dresser drawer. This Jewish ritual object is supposed to be fastened to the doorpost of a Jewish house in accordance with ancient law. It marks the home of a Jewish family, and for many also symbolizes the liminal space between worlds. I had intended to put it on the doorframe of my flat, but found myself feeling too erased and overcome by anti-Semitism to put it up. I hadn't been ready for my Jewishness to be so visible. So it lay hidden away, where I too kept my identity and sorrow under wraps.

One day, I brought Maja's part to rehearsal and asked her to read it out loud so we could hear her story from her own words. She was too scared and suggested that one of the actresses read it instead. As Kasia read, Maja wept and wept. She was still weeping the next day. But something was clearing. Something invisible and beautiful. Trust between the girls and actresses continued to deepen as we spent more time together. Bonds developed between each girl and the actress who was learning her part. Yet it was still a rollercoaster ride. Some days, the girls were reticent and sad, hiding behind one another. Other days, we'd find them in front of the bathroom mirror, deftly making up their eyes with gobs of liner and mascara, and singing as they waited for rehearsal to begin. We never knew what we'd face.

I decided to use the actresses to create a scene about what it had been like to be a teenage runaway. To develop it, I had the girls walk us through their experiences, describing the colors and sensations of streets, the smells and sounds of cold and wet. They told us about stealing food, smoking weed, drinking, and running from police. They told us what it felt like at night to have no safe place to lay their heads down, to run in the underground, to sleep under bridges. Together we created a structure for the scene, which I then rehearsed with the actresses separately. I was able to ask the actresses to push themselves physically in ways I never could have done with the girls. Accompanied by loud music, they ran through the space with wild abandon, spinning, changing direction, and almost crashing into each other with out-of-control fear, stopping only to catch their breath, or stare vacantly out into space. I had them run until darkness, hunger, and exhaustion took over. When the girls watched the scene for the first time, they were enthralled and excited. These were their stories coming alive. Someone was walking in their shoes, giving them voice. Bearing witness.

They watched Halinka rehearse her part, and slowly the others, too, decided to try to perform. All but Beata.

I'll Catch Your Wing

Beata was the only one of the girls who had never spoken about what happened to her during her childhood. A thin girl who wore wide circles of kohl black eyeliner around her eyes, she often got in trouble for breaking rules, sneaking out after curfew, drinking, or not doing her chores. There was an air of fragile brittleness about her. While interviewing her, when we'd get close to any dark emotional content, she'd stop herself. So rather than push, I encouraged her to talk about what her story felt like. I asked her to draw her story, and to describe the drawing in words to us. From those words, I scripted her part:

> My story is invisible
> It's etched in my heart…
> It has a past…
> Has been beaten and bruised
> My story has holes…
> You can see it in my eyes
> The ones that can't see out…

My story hasn't been born yet
I keep it safe inside...
This much I can say:
My home life was a tragedy...
There are many things about which I do not speak
Seen by a young girl's eyes
Imprinted memories
That no child should ever receive

I am a flower rooted from the dark
Rising through the concrete cracks
My petals opening, revealing
Two big green eyes rimmed with black that scream:
I'll never be stepped on again...

Beata began drinking again and dropped out of our project a month or two before the first performance. Although I was really upset to lose her, I realized that she wasn't ready emotionally and would never have been able to keep her commitment to the group, to show up on time, ready to work hard at each rehearsal. But not wanting to totally give up on all the work we'd done together, I asked her how she'd feel if one of the actresses played her part. She wanted that, and would still come to rehearsals, although sporadically. One day, I was struggling with how to end the runaway scene. The girls and I were watching the actresses run and speak their lines, each finally huddled in her own sleeping place, waking up after a long night on the streets. I didn't know where to take it next. So I directed the girls to take over the actresses' parts and waited to see what they would spontaneously do next. They began comforting each other, reaching for each other's hands. I asked them to slowly get up and form a group center stage. They spontaneously put their arms around each other and rested their heads on each other's shoulders like they always did. I asked them to talk about how they were feeling. Beata:

Sometimes when I cry I don't want anyone to comfort me.
I don't want anyone to tell me that "It will be OK."
It makes me feel more helpless.
I don't want anyone to feel sorry for me.
I remember my mother telling me:

"It's not the one who dances with you
It's not the one who laughs with you
It's the one who cries with you. She is your friend."

That last line, "It's the one who cries with you. She is your friend," became the "medicine" of the show for me. We couldn't fix the past, we couldn't take away the girls' sorrow or scars, but we could celebrate their love and connection to each other. We could hold their friendships up to the light, friendships they might never have experienced, were they not living and healing together in this school for girls like themselves. Our composer wrote a tender and beautiful song that expressed their incredible bonds of sisterhood. My favorite line was: "I'll catch your wing when you fall."

Eventually, all but Beata performed. The girls were magnificent. They grew with each rehearsal and each performance. Opening night they were received by an audience of 350 teachers, social service providers, families, and the members of the general arts community, who were standing, clapping, and crying. The girls seemed to have become women right before our eyes.

Mezuzah

My last night there, the girls were celebrating with the team in my apartment. They were crying and didn't want to say their final goodbyes. We joked, "They stand at the doorway—they don't leave." I laughed with Halinka and then I realized that at this very instant she was standing in the living room, I was in the hall, and we were talking under the lintel separating the two. We were in the doorway. I knew that she was talking in Polish and me in English, but we understood each other perfectly. Suddenly I had a vision of the mezuzah and the liminal transition between worlds that it represents. I took it out from the drawer, unwrapped it, and held it out to her. We both touched it as we stood between the rooms. I had chills, and was flooded with feelings that seemed too big to contain. We were meeting in that boundaryless place between countries, language, and time. She had crossed through the threshold of womanhood and had stood proud, voicing her own story for the world to hear. I had come back to the land of my ancestors. Halinka, a runaway girl from a Catholic background, held the sacred mezuzah that houses the words "God is one." In that instant, we too became one. We held each other in a long, swaying hug, crying. And then...I was on a plane flying back to the United States. Back to my old life in the newer country.

CHAPTER 8

My Neighborhood is a Cemetery

Inner-city Violence

PHOTO © ED SEIZ

Back in Philadelphia I was in between projects, waiting for funding for TOVA, waiting for inspiration, and waiting for a new clear direction. It was the winter of 2004, and as I tried to discern what was next, another violent tragedy rocked the city. Faheem Childs, a ten-year-old boy, was killed by crossfire in the schoolyard on his way to his third grade class. It was one of way too many violent deaths of young people in Philadelphia that year, and for some reason, this one was the one that galvanized the city. I don't know if it was the fact that he'd been killed at school, or the picture of his hauntingly beautiful eyes shown in the media, but once I read about the murder, a huge wave of grief and propulsion of energy engulfed me.

I went to a peace march in his honor where we walked through the drug-infested streets near where he died. Mothers with grief in their eyes held posters, each one with a picture of their murdered son or daughter. There was loss in the air. We walked past gray and brown areas of debris and decay—a death march that called up memories of Majdanek. I remember that the shocking thing for me was that, in a sea of people, I could have counted the number of white people on both hands. Why weren't white mothers everywhere also up in arms? Why weren't we all outraged into action?

I knew then that this would be my next project. I wanted to hear the stories of mothers who'd lost children to violence. Their eyes haunted me, as did the sense that they were the ones who had the motivation and credibility to help end this unbearable cycle. I had worked with mothers of prisoners, and I thought too of their grief and loss. Their children were also part of the fabric of these stories, and as their parents, they too suffered unbearable loss and shame. And in thinking about what could possibly be the medicine in this story, I thought of the men I'd worked with in the prison. Men who'd once been caught up in the street life of violence that was still causing so much tragedy and loss, but men who'd deeply transformed and were doing everything in their power to be part of the solution. I thought if I could bring these disparate groups together, something very potent and healing could happen. I knew that I wouldn't be able to video or tour with men currently incarcerated, but recently released prisoners who were dedicating their lives to peaceful solutions to street violence could bring a depth and sense of hope and possibility to the project.

Before beginning, I went to the state capitol to meet with the Victim Advocate, hoping she would be able to point me towards some potential performers. But she was skeptical of the project, telling me that I shouldn't bring together people who had committed crimes with crime victims. She didn't even believe it would be good to bring mothers whose children had committed violence together with mothers who'd lost children to murder. She believed that the victims wouldn't feel safe. I knew her thinking was way too small and that we needed to break past boundaries of victim and perpetrator into the larger issues of violence, loss, healing, and redemption. I believed strongly that the very act of bringing these people together to deeply listen and support each other would be a step towards a model of restoration of justice and healing.

Deep in my faith was the knowledge that I'd recently interviewed Victoria and her two daughters—a family who'd lost their only son and brother, Emir, to murder. I'd heard them weep with anguish, anger, and sorrow. And I'd also heard Victoria express deep empathy for the mother of the man who'd killed Emir. She cried: "When the mother of the man who killed my son heard the verdict 'life,' she screamed. It was the same scream that came out of me when I found out that Emir had been killed. Nobody won." Hearing her speak, I knew she could inspire us all. She would be one of the linchpins of the cast.

In this early research stage, I'd also interviewed men who had recently been released from prison. I was able to meet them through prisoner community groups that that were familiar with Theatre of Witness from *Living with Life*. One of the first men I met was Hakim, a man who'd spent more than 40 years behind bars doing both state and federal time for very serious violent offenses. Hakim is a large and strong man, and at our initial meeting, I was a bit fearful of him. Now I would say that I would lay down my life for this man without blinking an eye.

There aren't very many times in this world when we get to really walk beside someone, accompanying them on a journey of deep emotional content. For some inexplicable reason, Hakim, a large, black Muslim man, and me, a small, white Jewish woman, made a spiritual connection of trust and love that I'll be forever grateful for. I spent time listening to him tell me of his life. He mined stories of his childhood and those of his father: the ancestral pain and anger following the lynching of his father's cousin, the retaliatory rampage his male family members made on 30 white people, and his father's escape up north and change of identity. Knowing this familial legacy helped Hakim understand its relationship to his own relentless experiences of racism, gang wars, and savage beatings by police. All of this fueled a burning rage that turned his life into one hell-bent on destruction. I listened as though my life depended on it.

> I caused a lot of pain to a lot of people.
> I did horrible and despicable things both in and out of jail.
> I stood over people—they be pleading for me to stop
> and I wouldn't stop. I wouldn't stop.
> I don't know where that comes from. It sounds like I'm a beast.
> I'm not a beast, but when that rage takes hold,
> you're no longer thinking.
> You go to a primitive place in your consciousness and all rational
> and humane stuff goes down somewhere where it can't take hold.
>
> It's not an easy thing to talk about this stuff.
> If you have any soul, you never forget.
> The faces of those I hurt will haunt me till the day I die.
> I wish I could ask for forgiveness, but it's too late.
> There are some things you can never atone for.

We cried together. Mostly I just listened. To say these stories were shocking would be an understatement. But there was something deeply moving for me about just bearing witness.

> In total I've spent 40 years in the penitentiary.
> At one point I did 20 straight years.
> Many of them in solitary.
> I've seen some of the most horrible things on the face of the earth.
> I saw a man stabbed to death in front of his cell and all I could do
> was scream and shake the bars. Vicious stuff.
> I dreamed nightly of detailed and graphic revenge.
> That's what prison is—a vicious, abnormal place.
> I don't ever want to go back.
> I don't want nobody to spend the rest of their life in there, 'cause
> for someone to be sentenced for the rest of their life is to say that
> God can't change hearts and I know he changed mine.
> That urge and willingness to hurt someone—

I don't know when and how it disappeared, but it's gone.
I don't know of any man who was changed for the good by prison.
For those of us who turned our lives around, it was in spite of the
horrors we saw and became while behind those bars of inhumanity.
I still can't pinpoint what helped me make the turn.
Maybe it was studying and obeying the tenets of Islam.
Maybe it was finally taking an accounting of my wrongdoings.
Maybe it was just getting older.
Or maybe it was God's grace.
All I know is that I no longer am governed by a rage I can't control.
I learned to exchange my dark revengeful fantasies for thoughts
about my love for my children.
I write poetry. I read, pray to Allah. And I hang with good people.
Finding those people on the inside was key.
They inspired me and kept me on the road to healing...

Every good and positive thing I do now is to make up for the
wrong I did to people. I'm working for my redemption—
giving back in terms of what I took away.

One of the many things I've learned from Hakim and other
prisoners who've done deep accountability and transformational
work is the extraordinary power of redemption. I see in him a
total life commitment to the intention of helping others. There's
nothing too big or too small that he won't do towards that end.
I believe that if we turned towards the men and women whose
deepest need is to redeem themselves, the strength and force of
their intention for good would go a long way towards bringing
real and lasting change to society's ills.

Continuing to develop the project, I interviewed people until I
had a strong cast of ten men and women: mothers whose children
had committed violence, mothers and siblings of men who had
died of violence, and ex-offenders. When it was time for me to
bring the cast members together for the first time, I wondered
how they'd accept each other. They'd all told me many of their
deepest and most painful stories, but how would they tell them in
front of each other? What would they reveal and what would be
left out? And how would we build community?

The day that Hakim told his story, I held my breath. I wondered what kind of emotional editing would take place and whether he'd share about having had his hands around someone's neck, in front of the mothers whose children had been murdered. I needn't have worried about his willingness to accept accountability, or his courage. He spoke as he'd spoken privately. We all had tears in our eyes, and from the look of it, a deep heaviness in our hearts.

When he'd finished, the first person on her feet was Altovise—Emir's sister, who is a police officer. She asked if she could hug Hakim and then said, "Thank you for saying what the man who killed my brother could never say." This was grace of the highest order. At that moment, I think we all knew that we were going to go on a big journey of truth and support together. And I knew that to the extent that the cast could have each other's backs, and model a true community across such obvious difference, it would be healing for audiences. As Hakim later related:

> I learned during the many rehearsals and meetings with this amazing group of performers that I yet had many, many mountains to climb and much to overcome. I cried as I had not cried in years. I had women put their arms around me and then draw me into their hearts, not just into their arms. This was new to me. I usually had to convince people that I was not a monster, yet these women knew I was not a monster before I had a chance to convince them. What kind of love is that? I cannot begin to explain what I felt, as this love and acceptance began to take hold of me. For the first time in many years, I truly began to relax and be relieved and be real. I will forever be in their debt.

Mothers Who Lost Too Much

The women in *Beyond the Walls* who had lost family members to murder, and the mothers whose sons had committed violence, shared among themselves a deep visceral understanding about loss and pain. Their stories, woven together, were a collective lament of grief about the violence and racism affecting the young black men of their families and communities. Different as their experiences were from each other, there was a commonality they all shared in trying to keep their brothers and sons safe from violence, both as perpetrators and as victims. And none of them had been able to do it.

Victoria:

When I was raising Emir…I thought all I had to do was teach him right from wrong, provide a safe environment and teach him morality. I always prayed to God to protect my children from harm's way. But I think there is no way to protect our young black boys. They know they aren't welcomed here. They want to be part of the American Dream but they think it's not for them…

Altovise:

My brother turned to what so many young men turn to—the street life and selling drugs. We all suspected, but we couldn't prove it. Even though I was a police officer, I could do nothing to stop him…

Victoria:

When he was a baby in my arms, I knew how to take care of him, how to comfort him. But now when I picture him, I see a teenager crying out for help and none of us being able to do anything to help him.

Altovise:

We got the call from the hospital. His pager had gone off in the emergency room at Einstein and the nurse called the girl who beeped him and told her that he was shot and didn't have an ID on him. She gave them our phone.

Victoria:

On the way to the hospital I knew he had died. I felt his spirit leave his body.

Altovise:

My mother asked the officer if the unidentified man inside was dead. He shook his head, "Yes." When we got to the door, she asked me to go in first. I saw his New Balance sneakers sticking up from a paper bag by his feet and I knew it was him. Then I pulled the sheet back.

Victoria:

I cried and screamed "What did they do to you?" His chest had four bullet wounds and clear fluid was leaking out. It was as if it was the last of his life was pouring out of his body.

Altovise:

We were looking at the exit wounds. At first I went into police mode and checked on everyone to make sure they were OK. Then my sister held me and I started sobbing hysterically, *"This was not supposed to happen!"* I was a police officer. I thought I could protect him. On March 26, 1997, my only brother Emir was shot in the back seven times and died on Rubicam Street. There is no way to describe this pain that never goes away.

Janet, a performer whose son was currently in prison, also had dreams for her son. But once again, the streets lured him in. Rather than focusing on the specifics, I was interested in his inner story— the story of his spirit and her story as his mother.

The day you were born was an ordinary day
On the cusp of a day too hot to handle
Pushing and pulling, we pushed and pulled
I got your weight
I pushed, you pulled, we pushed and pulled and you were slow coming into this world…

The day you were born the sky was yellow
You were filled with reds and purples and blues
Our house was too brown for the colors of your spirit
And when the gray of the world tried to shut you down
You muted your colors
Toned it down, to fit into a world not yet ready for the likes of you
And the pushing and pulling went on…

And the streets pulled and pulled and pulled
And the ancestors, they pulled and pulled
They gave us stories of resistance and transcendence…

And you heard stories of acquisition and conquest and the materialism designed to reel you in.
And I pulled and pulled and pulled

Sometimes I reeled you in and you pulled back—
sometimes I gave you slack

And the streets pulled.
And education pulled.
And racism pulled
I fought for your life
You fought for your life
A fist not of violence, a fist of rage
And the pushing and pulling went on

Until…

[*She turns to see the projected image of a young black man being arrested.*]

The night I saw my son's face on the 11:00 news.
Another young black male accused of homicide.

Listening and watching Janet, a woman of great dignity and poise, I found it unbearable to imagine one of my own sons accused of murder. I tried to imagine the cascade of emotions a mother would feel, knowing her child might have committed such a terrible act, as well as knowing he might now become a "ward of the state" for the rest of his life. I imagined great sorrow, rage, defeat, shame, and isolation. It seemed almost as unfathomable as losing one of my children to murder. As Victoria had said in describing the pain that the mother of the man who killed her son felt upon hearing of his life sentence: "No one won."

Early on I knew I wanted to create a scene with both Janet and Victoria. After trying out a few possibilities, the idea of a courtroom scene seemed to be most potent. From within it, we could explore the questions about mothers' guilt and how they could have protected their children from such horrendous fates. In the scene, all the women performers sat onstage as if in court. The mothers of the perpetrators sat on one side, the mothers of the deceased on the other.

Janet:

No one prepared me to be in the role of mother of a perpetrator.
No one raises their son thinking that one day they'll be in court
defending him for murder.
This wasn't in my game plan...
I know as his mother I must be accountable in some way,
but I don't know how.
I did everything I could to raise a well educated, strong, caring
young black man.
I taught him morality and about the importance of education.
I didn't raise him to sell drugs. I didn't raise him to be a statistic.
I certainly didn't raise him to be number EK4963
at the state penitentiary.

Victoria:

We ate dinner at the table each night. We said prayers.
But I failed in protecting him.

I didn't know how. He was 20, but he was still young.
When I saw him on the corner with his friends, I'd look at him and
he knew I knew.
Should I have gotten out of the car and grabbed him before he
became Unidentified Black Male—Homicide 126?

Janet:

It happened when he got to puberty. I lost access to him... I ask
myself all the time, what did I do? What didn't I do? As his mother,
I am guilty by association. This is something you don't talk about.
There are no clubs for mothers with children in prison. I had to do
everything I could, to hold my head up...

Suzette:

What criteria are you judging us with? Yes—my son is in prison.
But that doesn't mean that I have failed. People are so harsh with
their opinions.
The jury always ready and waiting.
Until you have walked in my shoes and lived with the experiences
of my life—
There is no way to judge.

I could tell you the whole sad tale...
I could tell you more than you want to hear.

More than you would believe.
But there are mothers all over this city
who could tell the same story.

I raised my sons to be eagles.
I raised them to be eagles even though I knew there would be a
multitude of pigeons squawking down here, who didn't have their
best interest at heart.
Who'd put them in directions that eagles would never fly.
I raised them to be somebody.
But all that I gave them and all the strength I had in me—
it wasn't enough.
And now they are caged up.
But I still want them to spread their majestic wings and fly.
I know they can.

Whenever Suzette came to the last words of her part, she raised
her arms out to her sides with magnificent strength. This was
a woman who didn't accept shame. She took back power and
anger and used it to fire the audience up with her belief in the
possibilities of her sons' majesty. She stirred up energy and I found
it to be a thrilling transformational moment in the show.

Unexpected Love

One of the beautiful aspects of working in Theatre of Witness is
when a cast of performers not only supports each other, but is also
able to create and imagine together. During my favorite *Beyond the
Walls* rehearsal, I led the group in a guided imagery session that
came directly from a quote from Victoria: "Sometimes I think my
neighborhood is like a cemetery, the houses like tombstones." I
was deeply struck by that image and wanted to see what it would
provoke. As the composer improvised music, the performers closed
their eyes and free associated about their neighborhoods, both in
the "old days" and now. I listened and wrote their responses as I
continued guiding them. I edited their words into a short prose
poem that was eventually recorded by Isaac, one of the performers,
and set to music. Later, film-maker Rachel Libert set the audio track
to the images she had filmed of children playing and hands slowly

falling from a Jungle Gym's bars. The film became the set-up for the performance—a provocative introduction to the context from which the stories emerged.

> …There are drugs in the neighborhood.
> We lost Martin and Malcolm and hope.
> Now Daddy's on drugs and Mama's got to work.
> Kids are left alone. Latchkey kids. Children raising children.
> Miss Lucy died. Her house is all boarded up.
> We lost Hakkim. Hakkim went to jail.
> Teenage girl getting pregnant—
> She's a mother, but she's a child.
> We lost Daud.
> The children are in trouble.
> Come home and save the children!
> You can't die!
> But Daddy's not there. He's in jail, or just missing.
> Children looking for guidance—joining gangs.
> There are locks on the doors and windows, guns in the streets,
> Trash and broken bottles.
> Children are lost.
> Don't die!
> Come home!
> Come home!
> Crimson rivers flood our streets, with the blood of our own.

Beyond the Walls was filled with countless acts of mercy and beauty. I remember one performance that was particularly emotional for Isaac, who shared about the crime he committed on an elderly white man whom he tied up and left in a pool of blood. After the performance he dissolved into deep tears that seemed to have opened the floodgates. Backstage, the mothers whose own children had been murdered held him close and rocked him and prayed over him. I will never forget his vulnerability, nor the generosity of the women who'd lost so much. They were all one—all healing and weeping together. It reminded me of one of Theatre of Witness's core guidelines: "The blessing lies in the wound."

Redemption

Just before the end of the show, Victoria spoke about her grandson Emir Jr. who was born after her son was murdered. She described him as waking from nightmares, crying, and afraid that he too would die of violence. Then as the music for the final song, *The Road to Redemption*, began, her voice rang out with:

> I am becoming a bigger voice for me, and my son.
> I see myself speaking first for Emir, then our family, neighborhood, the city, and the country.
> As the lens widens
> I become the voice for all black boys who are human
> And whose lives are not valued.
> I stand up for all of them
> With my head held high!

After each performance, people surrounded the performers, wanting to talk, thank them, cry with them. But perhaps the most surprising thing was that, at every performance, very young children would flock to Victoria. They'd touch her, hug her, and talk to her. Victoria recalls one young boy who looked up at her with big eyes and said, "I'm so sorry that Emir died. I'm going to be a good boy so nothing bad happens to me and my mother doesn't have to cry." Even though we'd made the production for young adults and above, somehow Victoria's part was like a beacon for young ones. She became the channel for Emir and for "all black boys." Her voice, loud and clear, was like a clarion call for violence prevention and peace. And the young ones knew it. We couldn't have designed a more potent corrective.

We performed *Beyond the Walls* over a period of two years in theatres and churches, at conferences, and in two prisons. Bringing it to Graterford—a maximum security prison outside of Philadelphia—was perhaps the culmination for us of all that the project could mean. I remember when we were finished, Alonzo, a lifer who'd already served over 20 years, stood up. With tears in his eyes he apologized to the mothers:

I want to apologize to all the mothers. I've been here 24 years, and we've had all kinds of programs with victims, but this is the first time I understand the real pain I caused. I want to apologize to all of you.

He then turned and looked at the men in the auditorium:

Please accept this apology on behalf of all of us.

Other men wrote reflections:

When you see 6' 4", 240 lb. black men crying, you think that transformation is possible.

Prisoners could see that humanity inside. They could stop and get in touch with feelings and see a place for themselves in the world. It was cathartic. An epiphany.

In these stories, I felt the pain of my own sister's murder, the harm I caused my own victims, and the damage I perpetrated against my community. This performance resonated with all of us on a deeply personal level because of our own families suffering the pain of crime and violence.

I loved it. I loved it! Please keep up the good work. Pray for me because I myself has hurt someone [who died].

I did not just see and hear this play, I felt it to my very core... Having been labeled the "shooter" by authorities, within my mind I was always able to justify my acts of violence against others. However, after witnessing the hurt and pain that was conveyed by those mothers on the stage, I realized that there was no justification for the hurt and pain that I must have brought to the loved ones of my victims. Never again will I be responsible for causing such pain to another.

On a more personal level, the moment that meant the most to me was when we performed on Martin Luther King Day at the synagogue that I'd helped to found many years earlier. The performers and I joined the congregation for the traditional lighting of Sabbath candles and singing. Then the cast, most of them African American, performed the whole show as part of the service. One of the Muslim performers, as always, wore her hijab and stepped forward at the very end to speak over the music.

> Will all the young people under the age of 21 please rise?
> We want to give you a blessing
> There are thousands of miles along the road to redemption
> No need to make that walk alone
> If you're tired there'll be a place at the table
> The gates are open, you can always come home
>
> Stay safe, stay strong, and know that you are loved.
> The gates are open, you can always come home.

The audience was on their feet, clapping and crying. This part of the performance was always deeply moving to me, but this time, what was thrilling and extraordinary was that we were witnessing a Muslim woman onstage in a synagogue, welcoming the Jews to the table in their own home. Who was home? Who were the guests and who was inviting whom? I know that many congregations have interfaith dialogue and sharing of rituals. But to me, this transcended all talk about difference and commonality. We had just shifted the axis of identity and, for a brief moment in time, we were all one.

What followed was equally moving. The Rabbi suggested we make a large circle that enveloped the room. We all held hands and recited Kaddish (the Jewish prayer for mourning) for children all over the city who had died of violence. When I looked around the circle of prayer, at all the beautiful faces of tears and openness—this group of Jews, Blacks, Gentiles, and Muslims—I was overwhelmed with the memory of a recurring dream vision I had experienced as a four-year-old girl, that when I grew up, I'd "do something about love." I was filled with a sense then that this very moment was exactly what I'd envisioned so many years before. Home.

CHAPTER 9

Steal the Stars and the Moon

Polish Prisoners

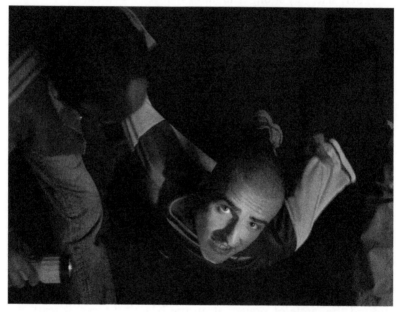

PHOTO © CRAIG CULLINANE

There is something unbelievably powerful about descending into the belly of the beast. I've always been attracted to the darkness, the hidden places, where evil and the shadows live. I have been moved by the knowledge that only by shining a light on darkness does the dark disappear. In Bemowo Prison in Warsaw, Poland, we did just that:

Tonight we are going to face the forbidden.
Shine light on that which we have locked up, cast away,
hidden and almost forgotten.
The prison within the prison.
The place where everyone is either a victim, witness or perpetrator.
Where we take all our mistakes, our rage, our sickness—
hide it away, turn out the lights and lock it up...
Tonight we ask you to open your eyes and see beyond the dark.
We are your brothers, fathers, husbands and sons.
We will light the way.

Zakazane Twarze (Forbidden Faces)

When I was in Poland creating the project with the runaway girls, I was invited to conduct a workshop with prison personnel from across the country. I shared excerpts from the film of *Living with Life* and discussed the power of creating Theatre of Witness with prisoners. The workshop was very moving, and the group subsequently invited me to return to Poland to make a production with prisoners in Warsaw. When I arrived, I interviewed men from two prisons, and then chose to focus on a small group of men at one of them, Bemowo Prison on the outskirts of the city.

At the prison, I was especially moved and haunted by two of the prisoners in particular. Benedykt, a former college professor, was quite erudite, interesting, and likeable. But he was serving time for killing his wife, daughter, and his wife's grandmother. It was almost impossible to reconcile this tragic and heinous crime with the quiet, polite man before me. I met him through his cellmate Dariusz—a tall and elegant man, who had been in and out of jail repeatedly for theft. Dariusz, who had studied yoga and meditation, was someone I could easily have imagined being friends with on the outside. With both of these men, I spent time digging through their stories, trying to find the nugget of gold, the positive medicine in the morass of darkness.

An Ancient Healing Story

When I first interviewed Dariusz, he kept his head down and his voice low, doubled over with depression and shame: "I am a thief. I stole from those I loved." I spent a lot of time with him in one-on-one interviews, hoping that one day his self-image would expand, allowing him to move beyond his limited sense of self-worth. I wanted to script his part, being true to his mind state as well as his story. But I also wanted to journey with him to find the place beyond his depression and guilt. I decided to begin his part in pieces, hoping a second section would reveal itself in another side—a story of grace or hope.

Part One began with Dariusz facing the audience as if he was sitting in a psychiatrist's office, giving monotone, disjointed, abbreviated answers to imaginary questions. Behind him, performers created a series of pastiches that highlighted some of the story imagery.

> They trusted me and I let them down
> Detox, depression
> I thought only of myself
> I did some awful things when I was free
> Again the cycle—prison—I don't want to talk about it
> Later, another marriage
> My daughter—another child left without a father
> I stole the money from my friend.
> My fault
> I still don't know why
> Make up for my mistakes
> I could have given the money back and I would be free
> Two children left without a father
> If our thoughts were a radio, we could simply turn them off.
> But there's no such a switch for the thinking.

Rehearsing this part seemed to bring some comfort to Dariusz, maybe because at least we were acknowledging the truth of his experience. But he still appeared quite depressed and I knew we had to dig deeper to find the more holistic story.

Dariusz often asked me about my meditation practice, and one day he suggested that I come in and meditate with a group of the prisoners. So one Sunday afternoon, a group of us joined together to meditate. The men brought in their rough wool blankets to sit on over the cold cement floor, and we sat together in silence. The meditation was simple, beautiful, and unexpectedly joyful. In fact, it was so blissful that afterwards one of the guards shook the blankets out, looking for some possible contraband drugs. He couldn't believe the mood shift was all due to spiritual practice.

The following day, Dariusz came in to rehearsal with his body erect, and a smile on his face. His voice was strong and clear as he shared some writing he'd done after our session:

> A day like an hour, an hour like a minute, a minute like a second.
> We cannot control that.
> Time goes by and that frightens me a little.
>
> I see myself at the edge of a precipice,
> and as I fall with my arms outstretched,
> I am examining my conscience. I am making a total accounting.
> I am bringing goodness into the future. Small slow actions.
> Not words—deeds. I want to help people who suffer.
> Both physically and mentally. These are my new directions:
>
> Don't avoid contact with suffering
> Don't turn a blind eye on others' suffering
> Don't let the awareness of how much suffering
> exists in this world leave you
> Try reaching those who suffer in all possible ways:
> personal contacts, visits, sound and image.
> Suffering will become real for you.
> In this way you'll wake both yourself and others...

When I read his words, I realized we could use this as Dariusz's second part. I had him stand at the edge of the stage with his long arms stretched up towards the ceiling, his head and upper back arched back, looking up at the imaginary sky. As he spoke, he slowly uprighted himself, opened his arms out wide, and drew them down to his sides like the hands of a clock. He concluded looking directly out at the audience. It was breathtaking to watch.

I knew, however, that something was still missing in his part. I'd brought a book of some Buddhist teaching stories with me to Poland and I began searching for one in particular that I felt might have some deep resonance with Dariusz's story. It is about a famous Buddhist master who had once been a notorious bandit who'd harmed scores of people through the years. At one point, he realized the great suffering he had caused and he yearned to make amends. So the bandit went to a well-known master and asked what he could do. The master looked at him and asked what he was good at. "Nothing," said the bandit. The master said, "That's not possible. Everybody is good at something." Then the bandit said, "Stealing." "Great," said the master. "I want you to go out into the night sky and steal all the stars and the moon and dissolve them into the belly of emptiness." And the story goes that the bandit was so good at stealing that in just a little over a fortnight he was able to go into the dark and dissolve the planets and stars into the belly of emptiness, and soon became one of India's most revered and enlightened masters.

When I told Dariusz this story and asked if he'd like to tell it onstage, his face lit up. So at the end of his part, he took out a blanket, sat at the edge of the stage in a yoga position, and told this story in his own words with great aplomb and strength, just like a master teacher giving students his favorite wisdom instructions. During the first performance, we could hear his mother sobbing in the audience. Later she was overjoyed with pride. Even a thief could become an enlightened master. We'd found a way to transform his own story of shame into one of the possibility of redemption.

Dariusz's part almost never made it to the stage in that form, however. It was an issue of translation. At every rehearsal and interview, one of the translators would whisper an English translation into my ear of what was being spoken in Polish. I took my notes from this initial translation, wrote the script in English, and then gave it back to two translators who then re-translated it back into Polish. This was quite a laborious process and required a lot of faith. I never knew how much of the rhythm or poetic intent of my initial English script was lost in the Polish translation. So one day I realized I should double-check the script. When the Polish translation was complete, I gave it to a third translator, and asked her to translate it back into English, hoping new eyes would uncover any discrepancies. When I read Dariusz's story, I was dismayed to find that it spoke about the thief going into the night sky and just looking at it, until the stars dissolved into emptiness. All the most potent imagery about stealing the stars and the moon from the sky was gone. When I asked the translator about it, she said, "But it doesn't make sense—you can't steal the stars and the moon." I didn't know whether to laugh or cry. "That's the whole point!" I realized then that I had to be much more careful, and that I probably would never know how well the script reflected my own artistic intent. More and more I had to do everything I could to control things, but then I had to just let go with faith and trust. A good lesson in all circumstances.

The Hell Realm

With Benedykt, there were other issues. Because of the horrific nature of his crime, we knew from the beginning that there was no way he could be in the project in a public manner. It would have been very hard for audiences to empathize with him. In fact, after the first few meetings, he stopped coming to our group as he had a hard time in relationship with the other men. But he wanted to be interviewed and I spent quite a bit of time with him, building a relationship of trust and respect. One day I screwed up my courage and asked him if he'd be willing to walk me through the murders.

He sat utterly still and spoke in an even monotone. The only thing that changed was the color of his face. I watched as it went from white, to red, to gray, and then back again. His hands rested quietly on his lap and he stared straight ahead. He told the story as if it was a movie script based on a distant character. I just listened and tried to remember to breathe as he spoke about the murders of all three of his family members. As I held the story, I tried to reconcile my feelings. How was it that I liked this man who had killed his closest family members without any seeming remorse? How could anyone do something like this and not be mentally ill? And if he was mentally ill, what was the difference between mental illness and evil? Was Hitler mentally ill? Did evil even exist? Could I love someone like Benedykt, while abhorring his crime? Could I hold the paradox with curiosity and the great tension of not understanding? I remember standing alone in my apartment, extending my arms out sideways to the walls. One arm represented my feelings of warmth and, yes, even love towards Benedykt. The other represented the horror of this terrible, terrible, violent crime. I held both arms out—both of them equal. Both true. Both impossible to reconcile.

About three weeks before we were to open the show, a reporter asked me about the crimes the men in the performance had committed. It was only at that moment that I realized that, other than Benedykt, who wasn't in the show, no one had committed an act of physical harm. Their crimes ranged from robbery to drugs. I realized then that the performance might not be as powerful as it could be unless we somehow included Benedykt's story. Still cognizant that we couldn't have him onstage, I asked him if he'd give his permission for Dariusz, as his cellmate, to tell his story, and he agreed.

Because Theatre of Witness is founded on the principle of each person telling their own story, I knew I had to find a way to have Dariusz tell Benedykt's story with all of his own questions, fears, and ideas. So he and I talked about what it was like having Benedykt for a cellmate and what questions it brought up for him:

> If you met him now, you'd like him. He's a quiet man. Intelligent.
> One who likes order, books, classical music.
> He speaks several languages. He likes to garden.
> He's quite handsome. Even one might say "distinguished."
> He could be a professor. A writer. Maybe even a travel editor.
> He told me that he had a normal
> childhood and he's still close to his family.
>
> I like him. He's a good roommate.
> He is diligent, punctual and very tidy.

He hates the sound of the television, and enjoys the kind of conversations that are hard to find here. Books, film, science.
As I said, we get along well.

Eighteen years ago he did something unthinkable.
They call it a crime of passion.
The kind of thing that stays in the headlines for weeks—
his wife, child, and her grandmother.

We weren't going to talk about it here.
We didn't want to sensationalize prison life or add to the prejudices that many people have about prisoners already.
For obvious reasons, he didn't want to show his own face.
And he doesn't get along with many of the men in prison.
A "lack of respect" on both sides you could say.
But he is part of us too.

When I spend time with him, I get confused. I don't understand anymore what is "evil," what is mental illness and what is just a temporary snap. I've asked him to tell me about it.
Walk me through it. Give me details.

I went back to my own experience of Benedykt sitting impassively while relating the story of the murder of his family members as if in a dream. I had Dariusz sit and speak in a monotone with his face impassive. The music pulsed like a heartbeat. The lighting onstage shifted colors on his face.

He looks up at the ceiling, slowly, methodically...
The marriage, pregnancy, separation, the change of locks on the door, is it really his child?
Pressure at work, he's out on the street. It's winter. He applies for an appointment. through work, but she blocks that too. He sees no way out. Nowhere to sleep. He's up for days.
It's all her fault. Without her, he'd have his home,
he'd be able to do his research.
Everything would be normal again.
In films, chloroform and vodka work. It's clean and silent.
But this wasn't a film and there was a struggle.
Somehow the knife from the kitchen appeared.
And the grandmother.
In the end, all three people in that apartment...dead.

He still looks at the ceiling when he finishes.
Only the color of his face changes. White, red, gray, white.
We are silent.
I ask if he thinks he crossed the line between good and evil.
Yes.
But he still doesn't really understand how.
He knows he's a good man.

[*Dariusz stands.*]

I understand nothing. Sometimes I think that in prison I am living in the hell realm that's so easy to enter but hard to leave. This darkness sticks like black tar making a mark that can be seen by you as well as others.

Who is speaking truth, who is mentally ill?
Who has just crossed the line?
The place so full of scars and wounds that one can only weep.
I understand why we wear masks here.
Without them,
our hearts might break open so wide that we would just dissolve.

Strangely, I did find comfort, as I think we all did, in descending into that deep darkness of the men's stories. Maybe it's because they were true, and when the truth is exposed, no matter how terrible, its very exposure already is itself light. *Forbidden Faces* has taught me to fear less in treading into the murky waters. Bearing witness to evil and horror helped me to trust my capacity to be open to the full range of life. It has grown me as a human being. And for that I feel grateful.

CHAPTER 10

Sucking Water from Mud

Domestic Abuse

PHOTO © MELVIN EPPS

A few years after *Home Tales* was completed, in Philadelphia in the mid-Nineties, before working in the prison or going to Poland, I was surprised to get a call from Carlos. He said he had been committing domestic violence on his wife Sofia, and as part of his recovery, he wanted to reach out to other men. When he called the domestic abuse hotline, they reported having no programs for men. So he told me he'd prayed, and when he did, my name kept coming up. He wanted to know if I'd make a Theatre of Witness piece for him. At that time, we'd just finished touring *Growing up Female*, and in post-performance discussions I was often asked when I'd do a similar project for boys and men. I'd always demurred, saying it would be one of the last things that would draw me—working with all men. But now I heard Carlos's phone call as a deep spiritual request. There was no way I could not answer this call.

So *Man to Man* was born and Carlos and his son Diego were key figures. In it, Carlos spoke about the monster inside of him that allowed him to hit the very one he loved most in the world. Diego witnessed Carlos's violence:

Diego:

Enough! Stop hitting my mother. You're supposed to be my father. Can't you see that you're just putting hate in me? Stop it!!

Carlos:

I look in my son's eyes and I feel so much shame. I'm so confused.

Harry:

And no one ever talks about it. Once the woman is hit, she walks out with a black eye and everyone is around her giving her support—telling her to leave. But there's a wall of silence around us. No one will talk to us. No man will call us on it and tell us how wrong it is. It's almost like a code.

Carlos:

And we have to look her in the eye the next day—and know we've done this horrible thing. To the person we love and said we'd protect.
Nothing I say can ever make up for hurting her like that.

[*Sung:*]
They said to be a man
here's what you must do
Never let them see your fear
and hurt them if you do

The fears ran in my arms
My fists of anger flew
and as the violence left my hand
the fire left me too.

During the song Diego and Carlos would stand, arms around each other, with tears in their eyes. I still can't imagine the courage it took for Carlos to publicly declare accountability for what usually remains hidden and denied. I always believed that it had to have been harder for him to stand on the stage and admit to committing domestic abuse, than it had been to escape the death squads in El Salvador, crossing the desert until Sofia had laid down in the sand ready to die. Carlos hadn't let her. This was the first time I'd ever worked with a perpetrator, and I realized that his acceptance of accountability had incredible healing power for all of us. We often hear stories of suffering and trauma from the survivors' point of view, but when we hear someone speak with shame and sorrow about the violence they've committed, it becomes a huge step towards restoring balance, healing, and justice. I also realized that we could keep listening to victims forever, but if, as a society, we don't learn from and address the needs of perpetrators, no real change can be sustained. Listening to perpetrators requires humanizing the perceived enemy, and is much easier when the perpetrator has accepted accountability and expresses remorse.

My journey with members of the Morales family began a whole new cycle. About a year after *Man to Man*, Sofia asked me if she could tell her story in a show. She did so in *Some Life on These Bones*, a project with eight women who'd risen after hitting the bottom. In it she shared about her commitment to help break the cycle of abuse passed down from her grandparents, mother, and Carlos. She usually cried onstage when saying:

> …But the violence from my husband Carlos continued.
> I broke down and went crazy. My children saw it.
> Neighbors, police.
> Everyone saw what was going on in our family.
> Then we got therapy, and I stayed.
> I stayed and committed to breaking the cycle in our family
> To help each other grow and heal.
>
> …I am a woman who used to run
> Who ran and ran until I stopped and said "No more."
> Now I stay
> And break the cycle.

At almost all *Some Life on These Bones* performances, Carlos sat in the front row with flowers for Sofia. His pride and desire to support her seemed to be big enough to overcome the fear and shame of hearing over and over the story of his abuse. I think being there also was a public acknowledgment of his complicity in her pain. It was beautiful to watch. So a few years later, when I got a commission to make a production about domestic abuse, I knew that it was time to bring their stories of the abuse and healing together. Sofia and Carlos were the first two cast members.

Raising Our Voice

The cast for this new show consisted of six women, all survivors of domestic abuse, and two men, Carlos and Evan. Carlos was the only perpetrator in the group, and many times he confessed that he wanted to run out of the room. He reported feeling the blame of every man who'd committed violence, and I knew it took all his self-control to be able to listen to the deeply tragic abuse stories of all of the women without bolting. I always pointed out the door and reassured him that he could leave whenever he wanted. But Carlos isn't the kind of man who gives up or runs from difficulty. He always stayed.

After the initial individual interviews for *Raising Our Voice*, as in every project we spent the first few weeks of group rehearsals with each performer telling their story to the group in whatever way they wanted. One day after hearing another heartbreaking story, Carlos wept in the group and spoke about his feelings of guilt and remorse. When our meeting was over, one of the cast members, a strong woman survivor of domestic abuse, cornered him and asked him to sit down to talk. Looking directly at him with fierce determination she said, "Carlos—it's time to forgive yourself." Carlos later told me that it was as if her words cut through to his heart like a knife, splitting him wide open. This was a woman who'd lived through horrendous violence at the hands of her husband and she was the very one urging Carlos to forgive himself. It is these great moments of generosity of spirit that bring me to my knees. This was a deep moment of truth and healing shared by both of them, witnessed by me, and, I'd like to believe, later felt by audiences as a ripple effect. Sometimes my only task is to get out of the way so these moments of grace can unfold naturally and fully.

Finding the Medicine

The day Sofia shared her story was really difficult. She spoke about the sexual abuse she suffered at the hands of her mother, the legacy of violence perpetrated by so many members of her extended family, and then the abuse she endured in her marriage to Carlos. We were all crying. Carlos went up and held her in a long hug and said, "I was supposed to save your beauty, but I failed." At that moment, chills went up and down my spine and I knew that we had reached the mother lode. But it was imperative that I help find the medicine in the story. I wanted to reflect back to Carlos not only the ways in which he'd failed Sofia, but also how he'd literally and metaphorically saved her life. Luckily, I remembered his story about when they'd escaped across the desert. I asked them if they'd be willing to spend a few hours with me in the studio reliving that time. And from the guided imagery and physicalization of their memories, Sofia's part was born.

> ...The war in my country got worse.
> People were being tortured and murdered.
> The government put a death threat on Carlos and he had to escape.
> My brother was in the United States and the only way
> Carlos could get in is if I went with him.
> We left our three children and walked across mountains and desert.
> No water or food. Only sand.
> My feet were bleeding. Men were sucking water from mud.
> I thought I was going to die.
> I was so exhausted that I lay down and wanted to give up.
> But Carlos wouldn't let me die. He yelled at me:
> "What kind of mother leaves her three kids and dies in the desert?
> What will I tell your children?"
> I was so tired I said I didn't care anymore.

> But Carlos wouldn't give up.
> He kept yelling at me until I got mad enough to get up.
> I made him promise to leave me as soon as we got to Houston.
> Then we were captured, beaten and sent to a refugee camp.
> I stopped speaking. I became mute...

She then spoke about the abuse, followed by:

> People say that because I was abused, I would become an abuser.
> Because I didn't have a father, that I would raise my children as a
> single woman.
> They say that because I was raped, I would become a rapist.
> But I'm here to prove to you that that is not true.
>
> I am a good daughter, mother, wife.
> I am a good human being.
> I have raised my family with love.
>
> No one can take away the beauty of me.
> How can my mom take it away—the beauty of a woman?
> No. No one can take away the beauty of me.

I had Carlos sit onstage watching Sofia's part, which ended with
some flowers being strewn on the floor. After she exited, Carlos
picked up the flowers and began.

> I was supposed to be the one to save Sofia.
> I was supposed to give her all the love and respect
> she never got as a child.
> I was supposed to save her beauty.
> But I failed.
>
> One day I saw myself in the hall mirror. I saw my own face—but
> it wasn't me. I saw a monster. I saw the face of someone who had
> been beating Sofia. She was hiding in the closet and the kids were
> screaming. I don't know how I got there.
> I looked into the mirror and I asked, "Who is that person?
> How can that person be me?..."
>
> Once I was the one to save Sofia.
> We were in the desert, men on their hands and knees, crying.
> She was exhausted, laying on the sand.
> Grown men were crying, trying to drink water from mud.
> She wanted to give up and die. But I wouldn't let her.

That was the closest I ever felt to another human being.
It was like we were one person, one breath away from death.
The only reason for my life was to save her.
I got her angry on purpose, because I knew that if she was mad
enough, she'd get up and keep walking towards our freedom.
I didn't care about my own self.
At that moment, my only purpose was to keep her alive.
I would have died there in a minute to save her.
I always would die to save her.

I look at myself in the mirror and I see what has to die. It's the
monster—the violent one.
The damaged part inside of me that is so scared of losing control
that he'd hit the one person he most loves in the world.
The part of me who has almost destroyed his family.
That part has to die so I can be the man I was meant to be—
a good husband, father, worker…

Now I want to reach out and help other men—to save their lives
and the lives of those who they love.
Sofia is more beautiful to me now than she ever was.
I see in her a woman of great courage, stamina and intelligence.
She has given me the greatest gifts a man can have—
three wonderful children and the love of a beautiful woman.
I want to be worthy of that love.
I pray every day that I will.
And that she and I can become old together and live in peace.

At this moment, Sofia re-entered the stage and came close to
Carlos. One of the other performers began singing the following
song while they danced, looking deeply into each other's eyes.

Like the snow that falls in winter
We learn to forgive
For when the ice is slowly melted
We get what we need to live

[*Chorus:*]
A fragile heart once broken
A gentle word is spoken
And we can love again…

We have this part on film, and years later, after countless viewings, I still almost always cry when watching it. I think it's because of the deep intimacy and love I see in a couple who have gone through hell and back. The moment when they touch their foreheads and slowly dance is a moment of such tender truth and poignancy that it gives me great hope that such depth of union with a partner is possible in my own life too.

Healing Happens in Mysterious Ways

One of the last scenes of *Raising Our Voice* was between Carlos and Evan. Evan is a social worker who worked closely with male perpetrators of domestic abuse. His part ends:

> Some of these guys walk in the door and I know it's going to be a long road ahead. A long road.
> But I never give up on them
> because you never know when someone's going to get it…
> You never know. Healing happens in mysterious ways.
> Sometimes it seems like nothing is happening, and then,
> all of a sudden, a man, a woman, a child
> finds that place inside of them where the natural tendency
> to be whole and good lives.
> They find that place of strength that lets them face the pain.
> And then they begin to do the work to grow.
> It's a blessing to be a witness to that. A true blessing.

I think about Evan's words so often—that healing happens in mysterious ways. There's something very humbling about the idea. It *is* all a mystery, and one that seemingly happens on its own. Yet at the same time, as Theatre of Witness practitioners, we can create an environment that supports this healing.

The Blessing at the Center of the Wound

We performed *Raising Our Voice* more than 20 times in theatres, colleges, community venues, and at conferences. But the most profound performance experience for me was at a small church in a poor inner-city neighborhood where we performed at floor level for the congregation as part of their Sunday service. The congregation had been carefully primed for what was to happen, and before we began, the pastor spoke eloquently and meaningfully about abuse. By the time we were near the end of the performance, most people were on their feet, clapping and crying. One woman in the pews was falling out with loud wails that overwhelmed the hall. Congregants tended to her with care, yet the wailing only got louder. We ended the performance and no one quite knew what to do. We were all standing in the center of the floor, with the audience on their feet surrounding us. We could hear crying as well as the loud bellows of a woman in the throes of some deep primal pain. Even the pastor seemed at a loss for what to do in this sacred moment. It was our composer, Niyonu, who took the lead and began playing a hymn. Quietly, folks joined in and the soothing sounds of people all singing together slowly took over the hall. The pastor stood center and began talking about the pre-arranged after-care from counselors that was available in another wing of the church.

It was at this moment that I fully realized that one of the most important aspects of this work is to create a container for communal grief. Abuse is usually hidden away in families and not shared in a public space. But it felt as if that particular church at that particular moment was ready to descend into the dark schism of that pain and grief. They were ready to go right into the wound to find the blessing of healing and connection. Our performance was the vehicle for it to happen. The pastor had understood the need for additional therapeutic support that allowed the congregants to go as deep as they needed. I left feeling deeply humbled and so grateful to be part of a moment of such potent honesty and communal ritual. Once again, the blessing was at the very center of the wound.

CHAPTER 11

Did You Understand What You Were Dying for?

War

PHOTO © MELVIN EPPS

I'd helped to tell the stories of refugees from countries at war, but until *Man to Man*, I'd never worked with soldiers who'd served in battle. When I met Tom, a Vietnam veteran who'd been deeply scarred by his experiences there, I invited him to join *Man to Man*'s cast. In the production we wove his story together with those of two other performers, one who was a conscientious objector, and the other who played another soldier and narrator. Their parts were amplified by the use of loud audio cues and powerful movement, yet it was the simplicity of Tom's story that always got to me. The following army songs interwoven with his script were the actual words he learned in training. I found it very painful to hear the cruel dehumanization that the army indoctrinated into soldiers, especially in light of the relationships I'd developed with Vietnamese people while making *Between the Crack*.

The Soldier

Tom:

Sir, my serial number is 13873449!

My M16 weapon is 1199965, 1199965, 1199965, 1965.

I was young and dumb. I enlisted. I didn't know yet what I wanted to do in college and there was a freedom in 'Nam you couldn't imagine. Especially for young guys like me with tons of energy. We had toys you couldn't believe—armored tanks, weapons, bullets. There was loud music, textures. So many patterns.

[*Sung:*]
Ain't no use to going home
2A's got my girl and gone
He's a bastard, she's a bitch
Re-up for another hitch.

I had asked to be sent to an operational area. At least things are real there. No "Soldier, put those bags down!" Plus, you got paid $150 more a month. In 'Nam I learned to be numb—to put up my shield.

[*Sung:*]
Killin' Charlie ain't no crime
He ain't worth a fuckin' dime
Shoot the mother in the head
You're alive and Charlie's dead.

They weren't people to us. They were wasps. The enemy.
And they were actively trying to kill us.
It's night and you're firing your muzzle at them and them at you.
It's dark. My head is down. I hear the firefights.

The sound of choppers.
Tracer rounds in red and green going 600 rounds a minute.
I pull the trigger. We nail three of them. Bedlam.

When the hit came, I felt it, but had no pain. Nothing. I'm in the no feeling DMZ zone. They sent me to the Philippines to get patched up—three weeks later, I'm back at the front.

Then the night I'll never forget happened. We were guarding an area and see a dead body turned on its stomach. Its leg and half of its side is missing. It's 100 degrees out and humid. There's a smell you can't believe. Rotting flesh. Our job is to guard the body until a squad is sent out to remove it. We can't touch it—it might be booby-trapped—a trick the enemy likes to do.

I try not to look. A long night. Then the truck comes, and they attach a rope to the neck of the body. It turns over. It's a woman, a 17-year-old girl. Her shirt rides up and I see her breasts. She's young, with stretch marks. A mother. Nothing prepared me for that sight. I don't know who she was. Was she trying to set a trap and timed it wrong? Did she just trip? Where are her kids? After I came home I went to bed with my girl, and had a flashback. I couldn't get that young girl's face out of my mind. Nobody to talk to. How can I tell this to anyone? I couldn't be intimate with a woman for more than two years.

[*Sung:*]
Buy some dope and buy some luck
Pay Charlie's sister for a fuck
Kill Charlie man or he'll kill you
Best kill Charlie's sister too.

My friend Bill died over there. When I heard about it, my reaction was: "Don't mean a thing. Don't mean a thing."

[*Sung:*]
Best kill Charlie's sister too
And her death will stay inside of you…

This was followed by an original song written by Tom, which he sang while strumming his guitar. He often had tears still flowing down his cheeks from his previous part:

The wind blows a cloud
Over her resting place
And you can't feel the sun
That's been burning your face

Oh no, did you understand
What you were dying for?

A baby is crying
And needs to be nursed
But its mother had died
Now the baby is cursed

When I close my eyes
I pray for the dead
Swim that river of sadness
For too much blood shed

The leaders among us
Said they knew the truth
They claimed that they loved us
But then stole our youth

Oh no, did you understand
What you were dying for?

And all of this behind us
Proves that nothing's fair in life and war.
Perhaps we'll all remember
Nothing's fair in life and war.

I keep going back to Tom's question "*Did you understand what you were dying for?*" and ask myself, "Who are the perpetrators and who are the victims?" How do we think about those questions when we're talking about the sanctioned violence of war? For those of us who vote and pay taxes, how are we part of the perpetration of violence? And how can we hold the often opposing stories of all who are affected by war? Tom's distress in reliving standing guard by the body of the young Vietnamese woman was palpable. It was the first time I really understood the ongoing trauma of post-traumatic stress disorder (PTSD) that affects so many soldiers, victims, and witnesses of war. There is no monopoly on the suffering caused by war. And it doesn't end when the violence is over.

Mother's Milk

Probably the most profound example for me of the intergenerational effects of war was working with Hung on *Two Sides of the Moon*—a subsequent project with Vietnamese refugees and immigrants living in New Jersey. Hung shared memories that weren't hers. They were the ones passed down from her mother who had lived through the war in Vietnam. These memories were imprinted on her, and just as real and traumatic as if they'd happened to her.

> When I was growing up in Vietnam, we didn't have TV or radio, and all the time my mother told me true stories from her life. I heard these stories so many times that I absorbed them like they were my own, drinking in the suffering and inhumanity like mother's milk. Milk tainted with poison.

Hung describes her mother's early childhood and her forced marriage at age 16 to a village boy. Then:

> One night, right after my sister was born, the French came to my mother's village and began terrorizing people. They called for her husband to come outside, and asked to see his papers. Then they shot him in the head right in front of my mother. An interpreter told my mother not to cry. Not to make a sound. She watched her husband get killed and she stayed quiet. The soldiers then shot at her, but missed, and the bullet went over her shoulder.

> This is all my mother has told me about that night. I know from my work with refugees that probably many of the women in the village were raped and beaten. My mother has not told me this part. My mother was 21 when she buried her husband. She stayed living with her in-laws, taking care of them, the house and her children.

> When her oldest daughter turned six my mother wanted her to have an education. So she found a relative to take my sister in so she could go to school. Every day my mother paddled 18 kilometers up the river each way just to see her. She often paddled in the dark. The French Vietnamese war broke out and there was killing all around. Sometimes she'd see dead bodies floating by in the river. She'd move them aside to get water to drink.

> Sometimes I feel so helpless. I listen to my mother's story and I feel guilty that I have survived and didn't have to suffer like she did. I feel guilty to survive when so many have died and couldn't be here.
>
> Growing up, my mother and I were always side-by-side, cooking and cleaning. She recited these stories over and over, unknowingly transferring her emotions and fears into me word by word. All the time we cook, she talks and I listen. My mother was so young, and she couldn't fight back. I listen, but can't help her.
>
> She doesn't tell me these stories to hurt me. She is just lonely and needs a listening ear. But the stories are too much for a young girl. I'm angry and traumatized but I don't know how to react. I can't verbalize the impact and slowly these stories fill me up as I grow into womanhood.

There was always something moving and powerful about seeing Hung relate these stories of her mother. I could see the trauma in her eyes, and in her body. Yet I also knew that it was liberating for her to voice these memories and get them out beyond herself. By speaking about second-generation trauma, she was also speaking about the intergenerational impact of war. It helped me understand some of the pain felt by children of survivors of the Holocaust. Hung was telling a very personal story, but it was universal in its impact.

Left Behind

One of the other young performers' stories in *Two Sides of the Moon* made me question all my beliefs about the Vietnam war. Pho came to the United States as an unaccompanied minor at age 13 and was adopted by an American family. He later became a US citizen, went to college, where he joined the ROTC (a college-based program for training US army officers), and later joined the US army. His view of the war was quite different from what mine had been, and it made me question my belief that we should never have been involved, or at the very least, should have gotten out a lot earlier.

> When I was in Vietnam I wasn't allowed to learn about the war. Since I came to the Unites States I'm interested in it. I watch many movies and read many books. I want to know why the United States withdrew from Vietnam. Many veterans tell me that Americans didn't support the war. Others told me that it was because Vietnam didn't want them. In my opinion, they should have stayed to finish the job. We could have wiped out North Vietnam. When they withdrew, thousands and thousands of my people were put in concentration camps or executed. They were buried in mass graves. If, in the future, I get to be a leader, I would never leave troops behind and not finish the job.

I'd always thought of myself as a pacifist, and had certainly been against the US involvement in Vietnam. But after hearing first-hand from the young performers about their experiences living in South Vietnam after the communist take-over, I must admit that I found myself confused. Clear-cut answers don't seem as easy anymore, and I feel quite humbled by, once again, not knowing.

After working with Tom in *Man to Man* and the Vietnamese performers in *Two Sides of the Moon*, I hoped that I'd be able to do more Theatre of Witness with those who'd come through war. I had no precognition that it would happen in Northern Ireland. But that was what unfolded next for me after one more deep dip into prisons in the United States.

CHAPTER 12

I'm the Daughter of a Criminal

Families of Prisoners

PHOTO © RACHEL LIBERT

Nothing remains invisible.
Nothing remains impossible.

Holding Up: A New Prison Legacy

Ever since *Living with Life* had been performed in 2002, I'd wanted to do another prison project in the United States. So when I was invited to screen the video of *Living with Life* at Graterford—a maximum-security prison outside of Philadelphia—I was excited. Right from the beginning I was struck by the differences in the atmospheres of the two prisons. SCI-Chester, a small prison where *Living with Life* took place, had been built in the late 1990s and was modern, air-conditioned, and had a quite contained environment. There was no lifer association, and the lifers in fact were not allowed to meet together. SCI-Graterford was a rambling old prison with long hallways, and loud overhead fans adding to the constant din. Unlike Chester, that housed only 16 lifers, Graterford had a large population of activist lifers led by a group of visionary leaders. I was struck by the air of freedom the men seemed to have at Graterford as I walked into the cavernous auditorium and was greeted with a big, warm hug by Tyrone, the president of the lifers' organization. There was an energy of vitality, excitement, and possibility in the air.

The following few years, Tyrone and the Public Safety Initiative organized a Crime Summit and then hosted the World Congress of Criminology that had criminologists from all over the world come into the prison to hear about the men's model of Positive Transformation and Peer Intervention that is intended to interrupt the culture of street crime, both within and outside the prison walls. I attended both events and was again struck by the power of the men to vision and manifest big and important projects and ideas. They invited me to meet with them to dream up a mutual project.

So from 2003 to 2007 I met with the men on a fairly regular basis, brainstorming ideas, and helping them direct a play one of them had written. Together we organized a prison performance of *Beyond the Walls* that further inspired them to collaborate with me on a new Theatre of Witness project. We just didn't yet have a clear idea of what it would be.

Then, one day, I went to an inner-city school to meet with some middle-school girls some of my colleagues had been working with. I met with four girls around a table in the library, and asked only one question: "How has violence or incarceration affected you?" I was overwhelmed when, almost two hours later, the stories and tears were still flowing. These 14-year-old girls spoke about absent fathers, rape, prison, drug use, lynchings, and murders. They talked of carrying weapons. And they grieved. I truly didn't know what to do, other than listen and cry. They had experienced more trauma and violence than I could ever possibly imagine. And they were just a random group of four who happened to be in the class that my colleague was teaching. I know these stories are multiplied a hundredfold all over the country. Yet, it's shocking that they are so little heard by mainstream society. I felt quite helpless and unclear on how to proceed next, other than trying to figure out how to conclude this deeply touching session. I invited us to all breathe in unison with our hands touching in a circle. And I promised to come back at least one more time. Sometimes bearing witness is all I can do. I left, shaken to my core.

That night, I went to a meeting at Graterford, and before the group gathered, I was talking with Tyrone. He asked me how my day had been, and I relayed some of the stories of the girls. He suggested that I tell their stories to the rest of the men during the meeting. When I did, there was silence and a few wet eyes. Andre spoke with deep sorrow and passion about how they (the men) were responsible for the brokenness in the lives of the girls, and that they needed to be part of the solution. That was the gold we'd been waiting for. All of a sudden I saw a vision of the new project. We'd make a Theatre of Witness production with the incarcerated men, and with children and other family members of prisoners. It would be about the effects on families of having an absent, incarcerated father. Our goals were to break through the walls of denial and justification that many incarcerated men hold concerning the impact of their actions and absence on those they most love, as well as on society at large. It would also give voice to the women and children of the incarcerated, whose stories are often hidden, invisible, stereotyped, or misunderstood. Our hope was to perform for the prisoners, the general public, families, legislators, and judges to show how sentencing laws affect generations of families.

Our plan was to perform the production, which came to be called *Holding Up*, inside the prison, using video projection of the children (since those under the age of 18 aren't allowed inside), and for the performances outside for the public, the prisoners' parts would be shown on film (as obviously they weren't allowed out). As we developed the project further, however, the Victim Advocate of Pennsylvania denied us permission to film the prisoners. So we devised a new plan that consisted of having formerly incarcerated men play the parts of the prisoners for all the performances outside the prison. This presented challenges I'd never faced before. I would need to have two completely different casts of male performers, and I had to figure out which women and children needed to be filmed, and who would perform live in which venue. But I was tremendously excited and I felt as though I had such wonderful support from the men inside. Now all I had to do was begin. Tyrone organized for me to interview about 30 men on the inside, and I met with more women and children of prisoners in the community. Then I recruited former prisoners I knew who I thought could effectively step into the shoes of their still incarcerated counterparts, whose parts they'd be playing.

Crush of the Heart

From the outset of the interview process, I was aware that there was a multiplicity of ways that families deal with the separation of incarceration. For some imprisoned fathers who had not yet engaged in deep reflection and accountability work, there is often a huge gulf of understanding between them and their children. I listened to one imprisoned father tell me with pride how well his daughter was doing in school. He brought her teacher's report to show me. I was aghast to read the teacher's claim that, since this young teen had purportedly stopped taking her medication, she was floundering academically, fighting in class with her peers, and having difficulty with discipline. I struggled to understand how her father and I could read the same report and have such differing understandings of its meaning. When I asked him what he thought, he said that he knew his daughter was just misunderstood by this particular teacher and clearly didn't need medication. In his eyes, she was smart, well behaved, and popular, and if he were home, he'd prove it to the teacher. I think this was the moment when I realized that this project could be a much needed bridge between the conflicting realities of parenting on either side of the prison wall.

But even for imprisoned fathers who believed they'd taken responsibility for the pain they'd caused their families, this project opened new doors. Here is Harun, a prisoner who during his more than 30 years behind bars had buried some of the more painful memories of his last arrest:

> This last case, I was out on bail. I went to court on Saturday morning while my kids were still sleeping. I heard my verdict, and haven't been home since. I didn't prepare anyone for the possibility of me going to jail. When I think about my wife having to go back home and explain my sudden disappearance to the children, "You're father ain't comin' home," it must have been traumatic. We've never talked about that day. And I haven't been home since.

After the project, he recently reflected:

> Doing this project made me more conscious. When you catch a case, it's an onerous task to fight for your life. To wage that fight while holding on to your family is almost impossible. You take a position that is self-centered. And if you lived a certain life-style prior to incarceration, you already neglected your family emotionally. In your incarceration, you compound that injury with abandonment, but, like me, you don't give it much thought, you bury it far down. Rehearsing and performing the scene where I leave my family and home to get my verdict made me relive that memory. Now, in my mind, I see my wife's face filled with fear. This play brought it to me how selfish I'd been. I let my family down. Since the performances, my family and I have much more substantive and deep conversations. It got us all the way down to the soul.

In interviews at the prison, some men understood the pain they were causing their families, but felt helpless:

It begins with a crush of your heart. A child looks up at you and says, "When you comin' home, Daddy?" A man could go insane thinking about that.

On the outside, I heard from many children that they protect their incarcerated parents from their true feelings of anger and abandonment. Here is one 13-year-old girl who speaks on video:

I'm mad at him, 'cos he should have been with me in the house and my mom and my little sister instead of going out with his friends. He should have been paying more attention to us and if he would have we won't be having to go through this. [*She begins crying.*] I'll say to the parents in jail—they screwed up... Their kids may lie to them and say "I'm doing fine." But they know when they lying to their parents, they know they can't take it. We're NOT doing fine. We really want to get our anger out but we're not going to tell you to your face. You messed up our lives. You messed up all that you made us go through while you are in there. You should feel bad. You should be the ones saying, "Oh my god, I'm so sorry." You should be the ones begging for forgiveness.

And a 17-year-old male whose mother is incarcerated:

My grandmother she's been making me hold on. I don't cry a lot. I feel like if I cry, I'll make someone else cry. If I showed all the pain I'm in, I'd be in jail. Pain is in my heart. It's black and empty. Real hot. And it's building up and up. I'm trying not to take the pain out on anyone.

Q: What is it like with your mother in prison?

It's tough. It's hard. Sometimes the anger inside makes you do things you don't want to do. It's like someone telling you to hurt somebody or do something crazy or say something. A lot of times I try to do other things and push it aside. I joke. I try to hide it.

Many prisoners reported seeing the damage they've caused their families and they yearn for an opportunity for repair. Said one father:

> My contract with my children is till the sun burns out. I'll never stop pursuing their love and giving love... But who am I? I have to say "I'm sorry" for all the promises I broke. My daughter's looking for the same thing I'm looking for—to be appreciated and encouraged. I didn't know how to be a man. I have to trust in God to lead me in the right way and bring my daughter back in my home.

These heartbreaking stories of familial separation and loss resonated with me. My two grown sons had lived most of their growing-up years going back and forth between their father and me. Although they'd had us both deeply involved in their lives, there was a break in the family that for me felt irreparable. I still yearned to have them back living with me, back being a full-time mother, able to repair the hurts the divorce had caused.

But opportunities for repair are often hard to come by. In the prison there is a code of silence, born from the desire that incarcerated parents and children have to protect each other from the truth about the crimes they've committed, the pain and anger from being abandoned, the perceived public shame, and the machismo culture of manhood that deprives men from sharing feelings and wounds. Many of the imprisoned parents told me that, before this project, they'd convinced themselves that they were being open and truthful with their families. But once they heard the true stories from the children onstage and in video, they reached out to their own children, dug deeply into their own wounds, and saw that there was much more healing to do. The production became a tool for performers and audience members alike to measure their own openness to truth and accountability with their families.

Erased from My Heart

Perhaps there was no more startling and heartbreaking example of the stark truth of a daughter's feelings about her absent father than in the opening film of *Holding Up*. These words came directly from a young woman I'd interviewed who, because of the secrecy of her father's incarceration, couldn't appear in our project. I'd felt these thoughts were so important and spoke for so many young people that I auditioned young actresses, hoping to get someone who could do this part with conviction and authority. I met Tamika, who immediately spoke this part as if it was hers. It turned out that, in fact, her father had been on death row. So we had her open the show with a film of her saying these words into the camera while sitting on her bed playing with her stuffed animals. Then I wrote a second part that came directly from her own words, that ends the show. Here is the opening:

> I am a daughter who has not been claimed.
> It's a secret I can't tell.
> Can't say,
> "He's a deadbeat dad who's been locked up most of my life."
> It's a secret that no one knows.
> I'm the daughter of a criminal…
>
> I'm nothing like him.
> And he's not me.
> I'm not his violence
> His drugging
> His street life
> I'm not his
> Duty
> Responsibility
> Or kin
> We have nothing in common.
>
> If we met on the street there'd be nothing to say.
> What—you want me to buy you some dope?
> You expect me to call you dad?
>
> NOW you want to know who I am?
>
> It's a little too late for all of that.

I have secrets to keep
And a wall that won't be pierced
I'm making something of my life
And there's nothing you can do to help.

So when they ask, "Where's your father?"
And I say, "Away," it's the best I can do.
I keep you to myself
A secret nobody knows.

You're a deadbeat dad
Missing in action
Erased from my heart.

Secrets work both ways. Many of the prisoners I talked with in interviews spoke about being kept in the dark about their own children. Paul, a gifted singer, songwriter, and poet, wrote this letter while serving a life sentence. I find it particularly heartbreaking and we created his part to include it:

I'd write a letter to you, my son
But I don't know where you are
I don't even know who you are
Or if you truly came from me.

I didn't believe you were mine
Is it my DNA that we share?
Or just your mother's words?
Sometimes truth is hard to know.

But I love you and think of you
I pray I never hear you died on the streets
Or meet you as a cell-mate,
In a fight over prison food, or as a CO turnkey.

Are you afraid of the dark?
Do you cry in your sleep?
Do you long for a father?
Do you dream of me?

What kind of man have you become?
Do you want to cuss me out?
Spit on my face with hateful words?
Of the hurt and angry child I abandoned?
Or maybe your life is better off without me.

Son—I think of that word
And I think of those years,
Decades that I wanted a son, daughter, a family.

You are probably the only part of me that will survive.
You are the only part of me that will see freedom.

I want you to know me.
Know who I am and judge for yourself.
I think I would have been a great father.
I want to: apologize for leaving;
Hear what life's been like for you;
And tell you what it's like for me.

I'm still looking for you
And I'll never stop.
And I believe that some part of you is looking for me too...

Paul followed these haunting words with a powerful and plaintive song that he also wrote and sang. When he performed, the pain was palpable.

Women Hold up the Sky

For me the powerful thing about *Holding Up* wasn't just the stories of truth from the children, but the incredible transformation that many of the men had gone through to become accountable, honest, and committed fathers and men. Nowhere was this more courageously modeled onstage than in the interweaving stories of Andre and his daughter Toya. Andre is a 56-year-old man who is serving a 140-year sentence. Toya is now in her early forties, but was 11 when he got "locked up for good." From the beginning Andre had suggested that I meet Toya, I think hoping that she might be interested in performing with him in the project. It was extraordinary to have them appear together in the performances at Graterford.

Andre's part begins with him contextualizing his life before incarceration. He talks of growing up in the 1950s and 1960s with "fathers who were working, but coming home humiliated by racism." He talks about "frontin' manhood" through drugs and street crime. He talks about his own 30-year addiction to heroin, both in and out of prison, and accepts accountability for the damage he caused his family. During this part, Toya sits behind him onstage, listening and watching.

> It wasn't until I was 45 years old when I wrote to my daughter and said, "Let me have it."
> She cussed me out for two pages.
> I said, "Thank you. If there's more, let me have that too.
> I need to know your pain."
> That's when I began to really become a father for the first time.
> Forging real relationships with my children and family that I'd only hinted at before.
> Up till then, I was still putting *me* first.
> Not thinking about the peripheral damage I caused.
> I failed those closest to me. And they're still paying the price.
> I'm not sure there's any way to express enough love
> to soothe the pain I have caused.
> And if there is, I don't know where to find it...

> The change for me came slowly. I was in my addiction, more than I'd ever been in the street, skinny as a beanpole
> and slowly killing myself while in prison.
> A friend told my daughter, "Your father needs to see you."
> Toya dropped everything and came up here.
> When I realized it was her, I was disappointed.
> I was looking for some money for dope.
> "What are you doing here? Do you have any money for me?"
> She gave me two or three dollars.
> "Is that all you got?" "Dad, I'm honest!" I said something I thought was hip, "I don't know where you get that shit from."
> I said goodbye and never gave it a thought.

> A week later I got busted and ended up in the hole. One night while lying there in the dark, I heard my daughter's voice.
> "Dad, I'm honest. Dad, I'm honest. Dad, I'm honest..."
> That was the first time I'd thought of what I'd done the night of the visit. I cried.
> She'd put her life on hold for me and all I'd wanted was to hustle her for dope money.

By that morning I decided "I'm done." When I got my hearing for release I said "I'm not going to population[1]—when you get a bed for treatment, I want it."

I stayed extra days in the hole just to wait for it.

In treatment I confronted my shaky identity and peeled back the layers until I found the Andre that was always there, the man who is truthful, funny, alive, smart, and committed to trying to make things better for others...

He continues, speaking about this commitment:

The work to rebuild our communities seems overwhelming,
but I won't ever quit.
I am called to do this work. Because, all of our lives are at stake.

At this point, Toya rises:

Dad, I wish you could have been the man you are now, back when we were all growing up without a father. I don't have many happy childhood memories, Dad.

Mostly you were living in a drug cloud and then in and out of jail since I can remember—here one month, and gone the next.

I recall those back alleys and bars where we'd wait while you scored and shot up.

Other than drugs, you didn't care about nothing—didn't care if we ate, wouldn't talk to us unless you were high.

Our childhood was filled with Swat teams knocking down our door at night, lots of fighting and you being shot.

Then, when you were taken away for good, Mom gave up on everything and turned to drugs herself. I was 11, the oldest of all of the children.

Everything fell on me. I had to be there with the kids—
get them up, dressed, off to school, fed.
That was, if there was money for food.
If not, I did whatever I had to do to get it, including things a 12-year-old girl should never have to do.
I could make 100 or 200 dollars and it would cover us for food if no one needed clothes or shoes.
When you talk of peripheral damage, you mean us.

---

1 Going from solitary confinement back to the population of the prison.

> We were the ones who paid with our bodies,
> paid with our childhood, paid with our dreams...

Toya continued, while looking into his eyes. Onstage she told him about her anger when her brother was arrested and she saw the legacy of crime continuing into her generation. She told him about her sister, in and out of jail, her children being raised by relatives. She told him that her brother claims he doesn't have a father: "The streets is my father." But she also tells him that she forgives him:

> I see how you are now, and I finally trust that you're not the same man you were before.
> I know that it hurts you to know your actions caused so much pain for us.
> I don't want you to hurt anymore.
> That's why I say we have to move on. You did the best you could.
>
> I want to bring you home.
> I want to take you to the beach where you and I can sit for hours looking out to where the sky and water touch.
> I want you to know your grandchildren.
> I want you to have a second chance
> You know, Grandmom always says that you're getting out soon.
> Yet, I know that may never happen.
> You have a 140-year sentence
> and we're living in angry and fear-filled times.
> You may never taste freedom.
>
> People say it's the women who hold up the sky.
> Some of us have been holding up for a long time, and we're tired.
> We're tired.

The first time that Toya came to the prison to rehearse her part with her father, we were all unprepared for the level of deep emotion that was ignited in the room. One by one, most of the men put their heads down; some of them were weeping, unable to speak. They had all heard Andre rehearse his part numerous times before, and they'd read Toya's script many times too. But as Andre later said:

There's a big difference between reading and saying. With reading, I was still able to deny the ugliness, but when I looked into her eyes and saw the pain dripping from her words, it was undeniable. It was shocking, painful, enlightening, and cathartic. I saw that the way I'd seen myself in relation to my family during my criminal years was a whole other world from what they saw. Toya's view was much uglier than I would ever allow myself to see. This project allowed me to feel the holes in my being. Through her I now can relate better to all of my children. It gave me an avenue to reach them. We could speak about how my absence impacted them.

That day in rehearsal, one of the men told me he had to go back to his cell because he was afraid he'd do harm to Andre. Hearing Toya say her part had so angered him that he'd scared himself. I knew that, because this man was articulating and admitting his fear of causing harm, and because he was voluntarily taking himself out of the situation, he'd be OK. I reminded him that he'd become a different man, and could handle the emotions without getting violent. And he could.

Performing this production in front of fellow prisoners, staff, families, students, the press, members of the judiciary, and the general public took extraordinary courage. All of the performers at one time or another questioned why they were putting themselves through the exposure of deep flaws, vulnerability, and the possibility of shame. But the responses they received from fellow performers, as well as audiences, let them see that, by sharing what is often kept secret, they were speaking for families of the incarcerated everywhere. They were giving voice to that which needed to be aired, named, and healed. The men took deep accountability. The women expressed their pain. And everyone grew.

Nothing Remains Invisible

I don't think I've ever in my life met anyone like Donald Hall. When I was in his presence, I always felt as though his love and light somehow rearranged all the molecules inside of me. He had made a drastic transformation from having been a hardened, cold, street gang member, to being one of the most loving and calm human beings I've ever met. Although he was a small man, many of the men told me that when they'd all been out in the street, they had been afraid of him. He had been calculating and revengeful. But he had a spiritual transformation while in prison, and his original death sentence was turned over to "life." He dedicated himself to helping others and creating a peaceful environment when violence was threatening to break out. He worked in the prison hospice and called himself "Loving Life."

> Not everything is what it seems.
> For most of my life, people were scared of me
> and saw what was wrong.
> Until I ended up being sentenced to die,
> only two people in my whole life had ever seen the good in me.
> But unfortunately whatever they saw remained invisible to me
> until my third year on death row.
>
> I was in total despair, having real bad anxiety and suicidal thoughts.
> I kept asking myself, "How did this happen to you?
> How did you reach this point where you did so much wrong
> that society gave up on you and sentenced you to death?"
> I was getting ready to kill myself.
>
> Then I heard this voice in my cell, "Donald,
> you have tried everything else, why don't you try Jesus Christ?"
> I looked around and thought, "On top of all I'm going through,
> I'm hearing voices. I must be schizophrenic."
>
> I thought I'd lost my mind.
>
> Then I heard the voice again and doing the only thing
> I could think to do, I prayed to God.
> "God, if you will, please come into my life right now."
> In an instant it seemed like all the anxiety and burdens I'd felt over
> the years just melted away. I felt a warm sensation throughout my
> body, and was led to pick up the beat-up old Bible that had been
> thrown into my cell.
>
> I heard and understood familiar passages in a whole new way.
> "In the beginning was the Word, and the Word was with God, and
> the Word became flesh and dwelt among us…"

I knew those verses wasn't talking about flesh or pigment

but about spirit.
I saw that things are not what they seem.
We are all spirit, housed for a while in these bodies of flesh.

Donald's part went on to talk about the hard work required to undo the hurt one has caused. Then he spoke about the impact on families:

Sometimes people think we can get away
from all the horrible things we've done.
But it's all recorded.
If you murder someone and get found "not guilty,"
you might beat the court case, but you don't beat the case.
It's recorded in your mind and it will flash back at you
over and over.
It's recorded by the people you hurt.
It's recorded by those who heard about it.
It's recorded by the universe.
And every act we've done or not done is also recorded by our
families and children.
They remember every transgression, and every absence,
every missed event, every angry word.
The work we do here to transform ourselves may never be
seen by them.
They may never believe our changes.
They may never want to claim us as family.

But we can't let that stop us.
Every good and caring act has the chance to change us all.
Nothing remains invisible. Nothing remains impossible.

Donald used to say to me, "Unlike the other men here, I know I'm going to die in prison. But I'm going to die the freest man you'll ever know." This small man serving a life sentence truly embodied all the spiritual teachings I've ever sought.

One of the prisoners in the audience later reflected in writing:

Thank you for bringing light in a dark place... They say that the truth will set you free, well today, the truth that ya'll brought set a lot of good men free.

Wake Up

I would be amiss if I didn't speak to the effects the productions have on me. Often times I don't quite know what a production is all about until after I've seen it performed a few times. I don't know if this happens to other playwrights or directors, but it's almost as if there's a layer of the unconscious driving much of the imaginative impulse, that isn't revealed until it has finished creating. For months, I hold the project in the forefront of my mind and heart, thinking, writing, interviewing, and directing. And then on opening night, it gives birth to itself and then belongs fully to the performers. At that point, my role totally shifts. I am no longer under the illusion that I have any control. The performers own it. They are the ones onstage, giving it their all, supporting one another, and being the experts, teachers, and inspirers for the audience. I am now the observer. Often sadness and exhaustion overtake me at that point. Almost always, however, it's illuminating.

The night following our première of *Holding Up*, I stayed up all night, going through the script line by line, deeply feeling how each line resonated with my own life. It was a visceral, physical reaction, leaving me rocking, weeping, and grieving for the frailty of our human condition. The ways we let each other down. The deep chords of familial love and disappointment. On a personal level, I felt the pain of having my children with me only half the time, feeling very much like an illegitimate, part-time mother:

> My mother can't cry or say, "I need someone to help me,
> to take care of me for once." She separates from her feelings.
> Everything that makes her a woman, she rips it out
> and puts it aside. Trying to hold up.
> If you looked at her heart you would see tears.
> Tears from the pain of mothers all over the world.

I was catapulted back in time to my father's remarriage after the death of my mother. I remember the time he refused to hug me, and his wife didn't want me in the house:

I am a daughter who has not been claimed.

I thought about all the spiritual teachings I was trying to practice and assimilate. I thought about the death of my parents, and of my former boyfriend Billy:

Wake up! Life is precious.

That last line was from Tamika's ending part—words that came directly from her. These words were scripted on a day she came in to rehearsal to practice her opening section about secrets. Unlike her usual self, she'd come in late, unprepared, and in a terrible mood. I was angry but was doing my best to stay steady and calm. It was a big challenge. Tamika kept talking and at first I heard it all as complaints. Then finally I actually listened to the content of what she was saying and began writing it all down. As I did that, I realized she was speaking unbelievable wisdom. All from a 16-year-old girl. This was the perfect example of taking what I saw was the problem (her rambling bad mood) and making it the solution (using her words to be the gold in the show). I wrote her part directly from that session, and we filmed her performing it. It was projected onstage with all the performers looking at her large, filmed image. If there ever was one message of all of my work that I'd want to have emanate forever, it would be this:

I see a world where so many of us are sleeping through life
Afraid of ourselves, afraid of each other, afraid to live.

We only get one chance at this thing called life.
Why not love everybody?
We only get one chance and our ride is over.
We can't stop and say, "Wait—I'm not ready.
I didn't get to do this or that!"
We only get one chance and then it's over and done with.
Wake up.
Life is precious.

My father was on death row...

How do you grieve for a father you never knew?
Who broke so many promises, and never knew mine.

I put his obituary up on my mirror
Next to the article about my friend Vince

who was murdered last year.
I keep death close by. It's my compass, my radar. My guide.
Reflecting my invisible scars, my invisible strength
I talk to death daily. And they tell me how to live.

Things happen every day, we never could expect.
Someone is murdered
A new baby cries
Our best friend moves away
Our father hugs us tight.
We only get one chance to live. Then it's over and done with.
But we have multiple chances to love, to forgive, to begin again.
We only have one chance to live. We better make it good.

I wasn't the only one moved by Tamika's words. The men in the prison often asked if we could play her film at the beginning of rehearsal so they could immerse themselves in her wisdom and emotion. It was as if this 16-year-old girl had a strange and mysterious power over all of us—her words a potent medicine for us all.

We performed *Holding Up* at Graterford, and with the former prisoners in many public performances throughout the Philadelphia area, at conferences, theatres, and community venues, and in other prisons. We also were invited to bring it to Arizona, where we performed at a fatherhood conference and on a Native American Indian reservation. In many ways that was the most moving performance of all. Prior to the performance, one of the elders offered prayers for the earth and all of creation. Then she offered prayers for all those who had served, or were currently serving, in the US Armed Forces. She prayed for their families. And she offered prayers for our country's leaders. Following the show, another one of the tribal leaders got up to speak. But he began to weep and had to pause. Hakim, who was playing the parts of Harun and Wayne—two of the currently incarcerated men—jumped down from the stage and wrapped him in a large embrace. They stayed suspended in time for quite a while, holding each other and weeping. Once again, it was as if something big had broken open. I'd hardly ever felt so honored to be anywhere in my life.

Nobody Gets Out Alive

Sadly, in the three years since first performing *Holding Up*, three of the prisoners have died. It's particularly heartbreaking to see such wonderful men die in prison before ever tasting freedom. Ironically, Wayne's part of the show dealt directly with this issue:

> …A friend of mine said, "If you die in this place, your soul will never be free. Your soul will continue to be locked up if you die in here."

I don't know if I believe that.
I want to believe that if we really turn our lives around,
we have the power to become free in here.
I work in the prison hospice.
I see guys stay up for days on end
just to ease the pain of a man who's dying.
It feels good to know we can be there for someone else.
I've seen guys spend all their time trying to help out others.
But you can only do so much in here.
After a while this place gets small.
When I first came in here, this place seemed endless.
Now I feel like I could put my hand out and touch the walls.
The place closes in around you.
I made all of these changes in here and I can't do nothing with it.
I think to myself, "I'm not really a bad guy.
This can't be my end in here.
I don't think God brought me all this way to do nothing…"

[*Sung:*]
Some die by guns, Some by blades,
Some by overdose and Some by AIDS
Some by war, Some by disease,
Some by the suffering they feel and they see,
Some by design, Some by fate, Some by ignorance,
and Some by hate.

Don't matter how hard you try—
Nobody gets out alive…

Words and music by Dan Kleiman

I'd like to believe that Tamika's charge to make life precious permeated all of their lives, as well as those of us grieving their loss.

Alonzo Watts died of a heart attack in prison while we were still rehearsing *Holding Up*. He believed so deeply in this production and was our biggest cheerleader and motivator. We dedicated the production to him—a man of great humor, strength, and intelligence. I picture his laughing eyes, and hear his raspy voice rehearsing his lines with rhythm and jazz:

> It's impossible to describe the feeling of the street.
> You'd have to be a poet...
> Then there are those of us who are just part of the streets.
> The streets are in us.
> And we are the streets...

Jabbar Boyd took over Alonzo's part, which he performed with great aplomb. I still can hear him far down the prison hall, his voice booming while he wildly gesticulated: "To be or not to be!" He had a special hand-over-hand handshake he taught me to do with him while saying, "We got to man you up!" Months after the show had ended and I was in Ireland having questions about everything, I'd hear his last words to me with his voice in my ears: "You tell them that you broke down some hard-core prisoners and had them weeping, and if you can do that here, you can do that there." Jabbar recently died of cancer in prison and I miss everything about him.

And lastly, Donald Hall died in prison in 2011. He taught me more about transformation and love than anyone I know. And I do believe that he did die the freest man I'll ever know. I love you, Donald.

Nothing remains invisible, nothing remains impossible.

CHAPTER 13

Beauty Born from Ugliness

Fathers on the Front Line—
Northern Ireland

PHOTO © OLIVER ORR

What do we pass from one generation to the next?
A war?
The remains of a war?
The truth?
A lie?
Or maybe a story, a question, a dream.

We Carried Your Secrets

I came to Northern Ireland very much an outsider. As a Jewish/Buddhist American woman who knew very little about the "Troubles," this outsider status held me in good stead. I wasn't Catholic, Protestant, British, or Irish and I had no stakes in the conflict. I came to listen, learn, bear witness, connect, and, I hoped, help to give voice to some of the hidden stories. I didn't know that I would also come to heal myself too.

In many ways it was a total miracle that the opportunity to work in Northern Ireland ever came my way. Ever since my second project in Poland I'd wanted to work abroad again, yet *Beyond the Walls* and further prison projects precluded me leaving the United States. I found that running a non-profit organization, which I'd originally founded in order to contain and support the work, had become a constriction and a drain on me emotionally, physically, and spiritually. I had recurring dreams of me standing wearing a big black cloak, opening my arms wide to the sides, and walking out naked from underneath it. Everything in me was clamoring for freedom. Soon I was diagnosed with a serious pre-malignant condition in my esophagus. Yet I still couldn't figure out how to get out from under the pressure of work. I remember often speaking about not being able to see what was next. A friend suggested an image to me that described my state perfectly—skiing downhill in a whiteout, unable to distinguish mountain from sky.

It was only later, when I was invited to Ireland, that I realized that the reason that I'd been in that state of not knowing for so long was because the events that opened that particular door for me hadn't yet happened. It took a meeting in Derry/Londonderry (two contested names for the divided city) between my dear friend and colleague Sharon Friedler from Pennsylvania and Pauline Ross in Derry/Londonderry for the opportunity to present itself. Sharon told Pauline about Theatre of Witness and gave her DVDs of my work with prisoners and with victims and perpetrators of violence. Pauline, a visionary producer who is the founder and director of The Playhouse (a community arts center), passionately shepherds arts projects that promote peace and community connection. She believed that maybe the time had come when it was safe enough for people to tell their stories. She was intrigued with the Theatre of Witness form, and invited me to come to Northern Ireland to meet her.

Flying over Ireland for the first time, I was entranced by the green fields and meadows with flocks of sheep dotting the surrounding hills. On the train from Belfast to Derry/Londonderry I cried from the sheer beauty of the waves crashing against the sand and stone at Castlerock. Gulls swooped down as the train glided by the empty winter beach. The land called to me in some deep primal way and I felt it as an ancient feminine presence. Once I began to meet people, their vitality, warmth, and the depth of their life experiences called me too.

In contrast to the peaceful landscape, Pauline, along with Eamonn Deane from Holywell Trust (a community development and peacebuilding organization), spoke of the trauma so many in Northern Ireland and across the border in the Republic of Ireland were carrying after decades of violence. They informed me about ongoing sectarianism, paramilitary threats, alcoholism, anti-social behavior, and the epidemic of suicide. They talked about victims ex-paramilitaries, members of the security forces, people living with post-traumatic stress, and the pressure of so many untold stories. I realized that, unlike other Theatre of Witness projects I'd done with a subset of people in a society, this potential project would navigate an ongoing communal narrative of which everyone in Northern Ireland was part. Because of continued violence, instability, and sense of distrust among people, the stakes would be very high.

As part of that first visit, Pauline suggested I go to the museums to learn a bit of the history of the land and conflict. I'll never forget the moment I walked into one of them. Upon hearing my accent, the woman at the desk asked where I was from and what had brought me to Northern Ireland. When I told her about the potential Theatre of Witness project both she and the security guard standing nearby became very interested and emotionally charged. The woman spoke about having had an earlier career as a clerk in the registry of births and deaths. She said it had been unbearable to hear the stories of mothers who had come to register the deaths of their children. She described people coming to her desk, crying in anguish and asking her for answers about why their children died. She felt totally unprepared to counsel people—she was just a clerk and had no psychological training. Often there were long lines of people waiting for her, many of whom also had tragic stories. She told me that she eventually had to quit the job because the pain of these stories followed her home after work and she had no way to defuse it. She was often unable to sleep at night.

Then the security guard described how, since the Good Friday Peace Agreement (in 1998, when all political prisoners were released), he walks down the street and recognizes the faces of people who used to make and plant bombs. Now those same people are walking about free and he doesn't know what to think. He doesn't know who has changed, who is remorseful, and who is still proud of the violence they caused. This old man got tears in his eyes as he talked about the wounds inflicted by brother against brother in this land of so much pain and trauma.

Both he and the ticket taker expressed support for this potential project, saying that they felt it was important for people to have the opportunity to share these stories that had been hidden for so long. That strangers in a public setting had been so open with me about their pain made me realize how much need there must be for people to have the opportunity to unload the burden of their fears, dreams, memories, and traumas. I was also surprised that they seemed so open to the possible healing that Theatre of Witness could bring to a post-conflict society. I was hooked, moved, excited, and terrified.

Luckily, I was in good hands. Without the expertise and tender care of Pauline and Eamonn, Theatre of Witness never could have been launched in Northern Ireland. Both of them had a deep passion and belief in the possibilities of this work, and were visionaries who were willing to take the risk of introducing this new art form as part of the peacemaking process. They each had numerous personal and professional contacts and were greatly respected by people across the community. The degree to which people were willing to meet with me and eventually trust me enough to tell me their stories was due to the regard and respect Pauline and Eamonn inspired.

It was a very steep learning curve for me. I came in knowing almost nothing about the history of Northern Ireland and at the beginning I found it almost impossible to keep things straight. I didn't understand who the various groups were, what they stood for, or the acronyms being used for their names. Sometimes I had trouble understanding accents and different usages of English words. One day someone gave me walking directions to a fabric store in town. He told me to go down the "hill," but I heard "hole." For a not-too-brief moment, I'm embarrassed to say, I pictured a hole in the center of a busy street with an entire other city underneath the one above. I was truly in another country, beginning from the beginning. I tried doing some basic research through reading, but not much stuck until I heard the personal stories in the interviews I conducted. These very personal experiences made historical events come alive for me and I found I had some footing from which to begin. I learn best by this direct person-to-person transmission, and slowly a sense of the complexities of these people and times began to reveal itself. I trusted that with Pauline and Eamonn steering me toward a balance of views and perspectives, I would be alright. I just had to be patient, make myself curious and receptive, keep questioning issues of balance, and trust my mentors as well as my own gut.

After lengthy discussions among us, Pauline and Eamonn invited me to return for a six-week research trip. During that time, I gave some presentations about Theatre of Witness and conducted in-depth interviews with more than 40 former paramilitaries, clergy, politicians, victims, members of the security forces, youth, and community workers. It was humbling, moving, and daunting. I quickly found that people seemed to be interested in this new art form of peacebuilding and that there was a hunger to be heard. I knew that I wanted to be the listener/creator. So when we decided to apply for a Peace 111 grant from the European Union and Eamonn turned to me and said "This is at least a two-year project—are you ready to move here for that long?" I didn't even blink. The "Yes" that came out of me was one of the clearest and quickest responses I've ever given.

Whose Eyes do I See Through?

Victoria:
I've been trying to understand where I fit in.
But whose eyes do I look through?
When I ask, some tell me about history, land and wars
Others, about religion, clan and tribe.
Some say it's about freedom, oppression, poverty and class.
Do we all hear with different histories coursing through our genes?
Different music in our ears?
Different colors in our eyes?

I met 23-year-old Victoria during that first six-week visit. She and I had both attended an event at Holywell Trust called "Chicken Soup for the Soul" where we broke bread together and heard inspiring stories from three people about the effects the Troubles had had on them. During the discussion that followed the presentation, Victoria raised her hand. She was bursting with questions and passion. She shared that her father had been in the Royal Ulster Constabulary (RUC) during the Troubles and that she was from Omagh, the site of one of the most horrific bomb explosions in 1998. With her father in the police force, she had grown up knowing she had to hold his profession a secret, and she spoke of searching under their car daily for bombs. She was a teen when the Omagh bomb hit, and although 33 people were killed in her home town, luckily neither she nor anyone in her family was injured or killed. Since she wasn't a primary victim, she questioned whether her story "counted." Did she suffer enough to have a story? Did only stories of suffering count? And to what generation did the stories belong?

Victoria's mother is Catholic, her father Protestant, and she attended schools of both religions. She has visual impairment due to albinoism, is a vocalist who is also fluent in Spanish, and has traveled widely abroad alone. She is a young woman who crossed many identity boundaries and I, along with many others in the room, was thunderstruck by her intelligence, passion, and ability to articulate her struggle about where she fit within the larger narrative of Northern Ireland. When the discussion was over, I immediately introduced myself and the potential Theatre of Witness project to her, and asked if we could meet. I was delighted when she agreed. I sensed immediately that Victoria might be the key to the project. She had passion, talent, and a keen sense of the questions of her generation.

> I have so many questions.
> So much was downplayed, probably to protect us.
> The word "war" was never used. It's not kitchen table conversation.
> People think that because we lived through part of it,
> that we know the stories, we understand the emotional aftershock.
> But we don't.
> We know bits and pieces.
> It's like trying to fit the pieces of a jigsaw puzzle together
> without knowing what the picture is.
> I want to ask my father if he ever used his gun.
> Did he witness brutality? What's his story? What's mine?
> When I compare my own life experiences with others,
> I feel as though I have no right to feel pain.
> No one in our family was killed. No one was physically injured.
> Compared to so many others in Omagh, Northern Ireland, and
> around the world, I have not suffered, and I have no tragic story.
>
> But why do we compare and judge our experiences?
> Why do we measure who suffered the most?
> None of us who lived through the violence here has been unscathed.
> We all bear the scars, both seen and invisible.
> I was born in the middle of the Troubles.
> We've been carrying the secrets of those who came before us
> since we were born.

When I heard Victoria say that last line while on an overnight retreat with the group, I realized that it would make a good title for the show. Sometimes, a participant opens their mouth and poetry emerges.

Music is My Only Escape

Victoria sang in a band with a drummer and friend, Fionnbharr, whom she suggested I meet. Fionnbharr's father had been a Sinn Fein councilor during the Troubles, and when Fionnbharr was five, his father was assassinated in broad daylight at the college where he had been an instructor. His family was convinced that the reason the case was never solved was that there had been collusion between the killer and the RUC (police). Fionnbharr hated anyone connected with the RUC and said that if he'd known at the beginning that Victoria's father had been in the police, he never would have been in the band with her. When I met him, I was struck by his openness and willingness to talk. But when we spoke about his father, Fionnbharr put his head down, spoke in a monotone, cried and shook like a baby. I'd rarely seen anyone so raw and open from the effects of trauma. And yet, I also had the sense of great strength inside of him.

> The 16th of September, 1991. I am five years old and at school.
> It is twenty past nine in the morning—broad daylight.
> Miles away, on a busy college campus, a college instructor
> opens his car door and another man mingles with the crowd.
> He wears no mask to cover his face.
> He moves just 12 inches away and calls out "Bernard!"
> Then he fires eight bullets from a .22 before
> fading back into the crowd.
> My Da is done.

Fionnbharr loved to drum, and when I asked him about it, he said:

> I have a lot of anger.
> It's easier to take it out on someone that has nothing to do with it.
> That's why I play drums.
> It's the only thing I can hit and get away with it.

> I sit down behind a kit and lose track of myself. I sit there for
> hours. Music is my only escape. I'm stuck being Bernard's son for
> the rest of my life. But music, that's me.
> It's the only way I'll be able to escape from this society.
> I don't want to forget about it, just not be trapped by it.
> There is no beginning, middle or end. It's never had an end.

I knew that if Fionnbharr was going to be in the project, drumming
would be his medicine. I decided that he'd drum onstage as a way
not only to comfort himself, but also to show the audience the
degree of his anger and pain. I wasn't yet sure what the form of
his part would be, but I knew that I wanted both him and Victoria
in the production.

Picking up the Pieces

During that same research trip, Pauline introduced me to Robin,
who was a former RUC officer and now a Community Officer in
the PSNI (Police Service of Northern Ireland). They'd met on a
peace trip to the Middle East and Pauline had been moved by
Robin's integrity and commitment to becoming a peacemaker. We
met briefly at a presentation Robin gave about community policing
during riots and violence and he agreed to be interviewed by me.

I usually conduct interviews in a neutral place, but with
Robin's busy schedule, we met together at a room in the police
station. My prison work had prepared me for issues of security
and I was somewhat less intimidated than I might have been by
all the uniforms and protocol. From the beginning Robin was very
open about his love of the military and policing, his commitment
to peacemaking, and the heavy toll his policing had taken on him
personally and psychologically.

During the 1980s and 1990s, Robin had been on the body
recovery team and had been on duty at two horrifying scenes. The
first was a major bomb explosion at a checkpoint at Coshquin (at
the army barracks).

> The 1980s. It was at the height of violence. We'd lost nine
> colleagues in Newry in one go-in. Explosions were so common

that I got to the stage of laying all my gear out beside my bed.
4:00am.
"Get your arse down here, there's been a major incident!
A bomb at a checkpoint!"
They had kidnapped Patsy Gillespie, chained him to his van
with a bomb loaded into the back, drove to the checkpoint
and then pressed the button.
There was a huge explosion that vaporized everything.
This massive reinforced building was blown to bits.
To make it worse, one of our guys in the observation look-out
thought that the building was under fire
and shot at his own foot patrol.
It was mass murder.
The police had no way to deal with it.
"Everybody, start clearing, whatever you find, document it
and put it in a bag."
I started from 300 yards away and slowly moved in.
We fanned out in a circle, each taking a triangular-shaped wedge
in towards the middle of the huge crater.
The place was littered with human body parts.
I found someone's backside in a field.
No front, just the cheeks.
Into the bag.
I worked my way into the middle of the scene.
Pick it up, drop it into the bag.
There was a brick in a pile of rubble. I lifted it.
Underneath was a human heart.
Pick it up, drop it in the bag
Pick it up, drop it in
Up, in…up, in.
At the time of the blast, there had been seven soldiers in the
armored personnel carrier at the checkpoint.
I didn't want to look at what remained.
I opened the back.
Nothing.
Not one shred of anything.
The force of the blast had sucked seven human beings
out through the viewing windows, each the size of a mail slot.
Totally vaporized everything.

Being professional, you learn to flip the switch. I had a job to do.
Nine times out of ten, with the plasticity of youth,
you can get over it.
But this was the beginning of a whole new dimension.
We had no preparation.
We didn't know how to process any of what we'd witnessed.

We had to account for everything:
documents, body parts, ammunition.
I knelt down reading a document and didn't notice
that the press was surrounding us.
They knew the rule never to show a police officer's face.
So there on *Derry Journal*'s front page was a picture of the carnage
with a little figure crouched down in the road
sorting through paperwork.
One little figure amidst all the horror.
That little figure is me, so it is.
You can keep pouring cups of water into a bucket,
but eventually the bucket will be full,
and the water will spill and leak out the sides.

Following that incident, Robin had spent weeks identifying bodies and clearing up the endless debris. Later, he did the same after the Omagh bomb. He talked to me about the emotional toll the two traumatic scenes had caused him. It felt to me like an important story that few people usually hear:

Two years down the line, as I began slipping into depression and traumatic stress, I was still trying to keep going.
But some of the other guys who kept going were going down to the bars. Others resigned. Some tried putting guns to their heads. Still others drove off roads. We lost more to suicide.
We wouldn't dream to tell people what was going on in our heads.
I refused to consume alcohol. I was scared to,
I had to hold on to whatever sanity I had left.
But one day I slipped in the kitchen,
and the glass I was holding broke. I burst into tears.
"I can't even get that right. Can't even hold a glass!"
The bucket was now full.

The counselors called it Posttraumatic Stress Disorder,
a nice professional name for Hell.
I was an ex-combatant, shell-shocked and in need of care.
Without rapid eye movement sleep, my mind couldn't file
all the images it had seen.
Instead, scenes were logjammed in my brain,
playing themselves over and over.
I could forget nothing. That switch was stuck in the on position
and I couldn't turn anything off.
So we reprocessed my eye movements,
and taught my brain new ways to file.
I went on desk duty, and took time to heal.
Heal yes, but forget no.
My ex-wife was right. I am no longer the same man.
I am a better one.
My memories of cleaning up after so much carnage changed me.
Omagh earned me the right to speak.
I've lived through the horror of seeing what human beings can do
to each other and I now believe that we all have our part to play
to turn this around for our children.
I will sit down and talk with anyone, if they will try to fix this:
enemies, combatants, students, elders, members of the military.
I will listen and I will learn and I am willing to do anything,
provided it doesn't involve the killing of another human being
in the name of politics.
We have to stop killing our kids.

I was deeply moved by Robin—his obvious strength and reliability, his willingness to talk about the post-traumatic stress, and his transformation from serving as a peacekeeper to that of dedicating his life to peacemaking. I wasn't sure, however, whether he'd agree to be in the project. How would he, as a police officer, respond to the idea of performing in a theatre production? I hoped I could convince him.

During those six weeks, I conducted a few long interviews each with Victoria, Fionnbharr, and Robin. We built relationships of more depth than I had the chance to do with most of the other interviewees, most of whom I only met once. Some of the other people had deeply moving stories, but either knew they didn't want to be onstage in the full project, had secrets they were too afraid to divulge publicly, or seemed still to be too traumatized by the events of their lives to be able to withstand the rigors of the Theatre of Witness process. Others I ultimately didn't choose, not because their stories weren't compelling or important, but because I had to balance sides, issues, themes, and personas in casting the production. I also had to imagine how the group would connect with each other and who would shine onstage. I felt confident about Robin, Victoria, and Fionnbharr and looked forward to getting to know them all better.

My time in Derry soon came to a close, but not before we began writing the lengthy Peace 111 grant application. Although we didn't know all of the particulars of the project at this point, we knew enough to articulate a plan and goals, and felt that we had made enough connections to feel we had a mandate. Those who'd been actively affected by the violence of the Troubles, as well as those in the next generation, seemed ready and eager to tell their stories. I flew home with hours and hours of interviews to transcribe, a full heart, and a great desire to return to this emerald island. My fingers were crossed that the grant would come through. And it did.

Crossing the Ocean

The months before leaving for the two-year stint abroad were a time of endings and deep reflection. The board of directors and I put TOVA to rest and dispersed 18 years' worth of work and files. Thoughts of defeat and loss ran through me as we threw out box after box of programs, posters, and press releases. I rented my house out, moved my furniture and belongings into storage, began treatment for a new and potentially serious medical condition, and helped my dear friend Carol die. Her death, which was lengthy, physically demanding, and intimate, was as deep a spiritual experience as I've ever had. The night before she died, I stayed up watching over her, as her body labored to breathe and her spirit expanded into infinity. She died as awake as any of us could hope to be, in the Buddha position, radiating love. Her dying process, difficult and ultimately liberating as it was, punctuated this time of chapter endings in my own life. The big leap of faith into the unknown that I would soon make became a bit easier, for knowing how beautifully she'd made the ultimate crossing over.

That last day in Philadelphia, I carried my two suitcases out the door, went to Carol's memorial service where I mourned the death of my beloved friend, and then hopped into a car to the airport. I entered that liminal space of night flying when one's normal life seems distant and mysterious. Time out of time. I awoke on the plane as the sun rose and sparkled on the beckoning land of green and a new chapter began in my life. Unlike my first trip to Poland, though, this time I crossed the ocean with the faces and stories of people I was moving towards, in my heart and mind. I knew I would be welcomed with warmth and care.

Beginning

> They say that it takes seven generations for trauma to heal. What will our legacy be to our great, great, great, great, great-grandchildren?
>
> *We Carried Your Secrets*

The beginning of the project was rocky. Besides needing to acclimate to a new country and immerse myself in its history, I had to sell Theatre of Witness to everyone I hoped to work with, as this work had never been done in Northern Ireland. I also had to create and develop an artistic team and deal with big issues of trust on all sides. Because Theatre of Witness was new to Northern Ireland, some people made assumptions about what it was, comparing it to community theatre, psychodrama, or Theatre of the Oppressed. I found myself often having to delicately extricate these ideas without sounding like I was putting these other powerful forms of therapy and/or theatre down. To that end, I gave as many public presentations as I could, showing excerpts from past work and talking about the process and our goals.

It also took a while to build a team that understood Theatre of Witness. It was a steep learning curve for the new project coordinator, interns, and other artistic collaborators (film-makers, musicians, set designers, and technical crew). Until the first production, none of them had ever seen this work performed live, had never experienced its effects on audiences, and had never lived through the ups and downs of the creative process with non-actors performing their own stories. Yet, they had to be the ambassadors for the work. All they had to go on was their willingness to take the risk and their trust in me.

For everyone involved, it took tremendous courage to embark on this new form of theatre that involved public sharing of these often hidden and potentially dangerous stories. There were fears about possible incitement of violence, and fears about reintroducing trauma. I too was fearful, wondering how to navigate my way through the complexities of relationships, politics, and history.

Most frightening, though, was that after we began the project, due to ongoing paramilitary activity, the security threat to police rose significantly. Very soon it became clear that it would not be safe for Robin, as a serving police officer, to perform live with us in certain areas of the city. Once word got out that a police officer was in the show, any member of a paramilitary organization could learn our touring schedule and plan an attack, hurting either Robin, a fellow performer, or an audience member. So we made an early decision to put his part on film and have it projected on a big screen as part of the performance, thinking that he'd be able to appear live in certain venues and on film in the others. In his part he directly addressed the reason he wasn't with us:

> I'm Robin Young.
> The reason I'm not here with you in person is that
> I'm a serving police officer, and for some people,
> this uniform can become the cause for attack.
> Anyone who associates with me therefore takes a risk, and although
> I don't mind taking that risk for myself,
> I am not willing for you to do so on my behalf.

The threat of violence extended beyond our public performances. There were also risks in gathering for rehearsals. The Playhouse presented a particular security challenge, as it is situated in an interface area between two contesting communities, and has only two exits, both facing the large walls that circumscribe the old city. Anyone intent on violence against the police could have been surveying Robin's entrances or exits from a position on the walls. So we varied the time and place of rehearsals, and my guess is that Robin probably took precautions that we weren't aware of. He did everything he could to ensure the safety of all of us. Soon after we began rehearsing, the security threat rose following the killing of a police officer named Stephen Carroll by the Continuity IRA dissident group. It became clear that it wouldn't be safe for Robin to perform live *anywhere* in Northern Ireland and we were all relieved that we'd planned for this contingency by filming his part. Ironically, his appearance on film added drama to the finished production and was a sad reminder of the continued instability of this contentious society.

On a bit more subtle level, trust was a difficult issue throughout the whole process. In a post-conflict society still quite divided along sectarian and political lines, trust was perhaps the hardest commodity to find. People often judged each other harshly, and struggles over power and resources were prevalent. I too had my own problems at the beginning knowing who and what I could most trust. Early on, citing all kinds of interpersonal issues, someone tried to warn me that I shouldn't work with either partner organization that was producing Theatre of Witness. This warning threw me into confusion and I felt quite out of my depth in knowing how to proceed.

I vividly remember speaking on the phone with my meditation teacher, David, about this problem, and he said: "Find out who's trustworthy." At the time, I was frustrated by this answer, thinking, "That's the point. If I knew who was trustworthy, I wouldn't be wrestling with this. I can't decode the signals. I don't know who's caught in their own trauma or prejudice, who is seeing things clearly, or even who's still involved with paramilitary organizations. I don't understand the layers of complexity. I just don't know enough." Then I realized I had to start somewhere. It was Eamonn Deane who I first identified as someone with impeccable standards. He seemed to listen without an agenda, and he was steady, clear, and smart. He didn't get his ego in the way and was extraordinarily generous in spirit and time. I went to him for counsel when I felt confused by conflicting messages and he steered me with understanding and compassion, often cutting through complexity with one simple and powerful statement. Both he and Pauline kept the vision and intention of the project in the forefront and they were a formidable team. The more we worked together, the more I saw how willing they were to risk their reputations for the good of this project. If it blew up in some way, I could go home with my tail between my legs, but they would be the ones dealing with the aftermath. They both lived in the city and had staked their professional reputations on this work.

But more than any of us, it was the performers who took the biggest risks. Pauline, Eamonn, and I may have felt responsible for the overall production, but the performers were the ones onstage sharing their personal stories. The ex-prisoners who had been in either republican or loyalist paramilitary organizations had sworn themselves to secrecy. Now 15, 20, 30 years later, they were going to reveal parts of their stories. If there were to be fall-out, they would be the ones taking the heat. At a residential with the cast early on during the process, James, a former member of the loyalist paramilitary group, the Ulster Defence Association (UDA), said:

> I don't think you fully understand, Teya, the seriousness of it. This is dangerous beyond dangerous. Having said all of that, I feel very, very committed. I think it takes a few people to stick their heads above the parapets. And if we do, just maybe a few more will stick their heads up and we'll get momentum.

I wanted the cast to know I took their fears very seriously. In fact, there were many nights when I lay awake, afraid that I was in over my head. Yet at the same time, I found confidence and faith in the guiding principle: "Trust the process." It became my talisman and I realized that, in fact, I truly did trust that if we hunkered down, listening, writing, scripting, engaging creatively, and speaking the truth, the process would hold us all. After more than 20 years, it hadn't let me down yet.

River

My friend, musician Roy, had given me an introduction to James without telling me much about him, other than that he was from a Protestant loyalist background and had a powerful story. James agreed to meet me at the Playhouse after work early one evening. I'd never interviewed anyone who was so apprehensive about talking. James wasn't comfortable sitting, and kept walking around, looking out the window. He kept asking me why I wanted "information," and was extremely reticent to respond to what I thought at the time were simple questions about his childhood. After he left, I wrote him off, thinking that there was no way this man would ever open up to me, and I had no sense of anything particularly interesting in his background. I couldn't have been more wrong.

A while later I bumped into Roy, who told me that James had very much enjoyed our talk and was waiting to hear from me again. Surprised, I told Roy that I thought maybe there wasn't enough of a story there for me to pursue. Roy just kept repeating: "Go meet him again—he has a story." So with a bit of reluctance, I called James and asked if we could meet again. He said he didn't feel comfortable in the Playhouse, as it seemed to be in a republican area, and he asked if I'd come to his house. Normally I try to meet in a neutral place that doesn't have the everyday distractions of someone's home, but it was clear that James wanted me to come to him. He lived about seven or eight miles away. I'd just gotten an old car that I was still learning to drive on what was the "other" side of the road for me, and I wasn't yet comfortable driving. Some deep intuition told me not to go, but I wanted to believe that I would do everything possible for the sake of the project, so I overrode my gut instinct and set out.

After two trips around a roundabout, each time getting off at the wrong exit, I gave up and went back to my apartment, made some tea, and tried to reach James by phone to cancel. But the calls wouldn't go through, and not wanting to give into fear, I set out once again. This time I made it around the roundabout only to get in a terrible car accident a few miles down the road. The breaking of glass and the sound of crushing metal terrified me, and the fear stayed in my body long after I recovered from the concussion and stitches. Luckily, the man who hit me walked away unhurt. It was only a few weeks later that I realized that my experience of this trauma was important in giving me a first-hand taste of how violence and injury stay in the body. My experience was so small and insignificant in comparison to the traumas that many people in Northern Ireland endured. Yet it seemed to serve as an initiation that I hope gave me a bit more understanding as I began the work of asking people to remember and relive terrible and tragic events. It also taught me to pay attention to trusting my intuition—it had tried to warn me, even though I'd ignored it. I hoped that now I could use it more fully.

James and I eventually caught up with each other and he began opening up. During our next interview he was sharing a bit about his life as a young man when I followed up on something he'd said, asking him about when his soul was touched. Seemingly out of the blue, he shared a deeply moving story about his childhood, crying as he spoke.

> It happened over 40 years ago when I was 11. My friends and I were crossing the river on a plank of wood over to the island. I turned around, and saw that a young fellow of about seven, named Thomas, was following us. He walked part of the way across on the plank, but then he started to cry because the waves were scaring him and he couldn't get back. We broke off two hazel rods for him to grab hold of. My friend Sam was in front, and I was behind. When we got to the center, both Sam and Thomas slipped off.
>
> Luckily Sam washed onto dry ground, but Thomas washed out to deeper water.

James spoke about running to the road and flagging down a car, but the older man inside refused to help.

> So I ran back where Thomas was bobbing along through the rough rapids into deeper water. I held on to a branch, my friends held the other end, and I waded in almost up to my neck. The current started to sweep me away. I could see that Thomas still was holding the stick and was reaching his hand out. His eyes were wide open. I reached out to him and my fingers brushed the tips of his. Our hands touched in the cold water—so close. His eyes were wide open, his red hair floating like seaweed, his face was as white as a ghost…and then he just rolled over and vanished.

> He wasn't found for three days. Life carried on as usual. When I got home, my mother told me to go up and take off my wet clothes. I went back to school the next morning, and nothing was ever discussed. The inquest came and went. We just went back to our lives, fished and played as though nothing had happened. But that day, the river claimed a wee lad named Thomas, and I still see his white face and wide-open eyes looking up at me over 40 years later. I wonder if that was one of life's turning points that changed me forever.

James had held the guilt of not being able to save Thomas, inside of himself since the day it had happened. Emotionally, it was as fresh as yesterday. In many ways this story didn't relate directly to James's involvement during the Troubles, but the pain and guilt he'd held all these years felt significant and foundational. I was also struck that he had been given no way to process the terrible, traumatic tragedy, and even as a youth he learned that he had to "just get on with it." That expectation that he could easily recover seemed in many ways to be a cultural expectation of growing up in Northern Ireland in the 1960s.

I knew that hearing the story would humanize James for the audience before they heard about his involvement with the UDA. I was convinced that it would be a seminal piece of the production. James told it at the beginning of the performance while sitting at the edge of the stage holding a fishing rod. A beautiful film of young boys playing near a river, made by film-maker John McIlduff, was projected behind him. It set a poetic tone for the production and led us gently into the stories connected to the Troubles.

For me, the river had particular resonance. Feeling so often dislocated and unsure as to which country or people I belonged to, I drew comfort and inspiration from watching the River Foyle intently from my top-floor flat of a renovated shirt factory. I'm a bit embarrassed to admit, though, that on my previous visit it had taken me a few weeks before I'd understood that it was a tidal river, and as such, that the currents flowed in both directions. My own sense of not being grounded had been so profound that early on I'd kept thinking that I had misremembered which way the river flowed: "Didn't it move to my right earlier today?" I began to view it from my window high above the water, and spent hours watching it flow back and forth, back and forth. But what entranced me the most was when the water began to change direction and the river both emptied and filled itself back up simultaneously. The water would seemingly part, with white lines dissecting it as it flowed in both directions at once. I could never track which way it had been flowing first, and that mysterious transition became a metaphor for me for all that was ever-changing in my life. What was coming and what was going? Could I be full and empty at the same time? Could this river that divided the city in two also hold the secrets of healing?

Losing and Finding Cast Members

During the six-week research trip I'd made to Derry before we began the project, I'd also met an ex-prisoner from the republican side who'd greatly moved and impressed me. I was struck by this man's integrity and willingness to take accountability for his paramilitary involvement that had resulted in a bomb explosion that had killed someone. I spent hours interviewing him, and he committed to the project, even suggesting that his daughter might also want to participate. She too agreed, and we decided that her part would be focused on the impact of growing up with her father in prison.

Fairly early on, the six performers and staff went on a weekend residential at a beautiful place by the sea. At one point, I asked the three younger performers to meet separately for a bit and come back and lead the group in whatever direction they wanted. They decided that they wanted to ask the older men questions. Some of those questions still haunt me: "What made you join a paramilitary, political, or military organization? What did you promise to do? How did gender affect you?" Their last question was: "How does it feel to kill someone?" I was struck with the bravery of the young people to ask these taboo questions. This was when I truly realized the degree to which the intergenerational secrets affect them all. The men all answered with deep respect and honesty. After such depth of sharing, I felt confident in the group and its cohesiveness.

But some time after our residential, the republican ex-prisoner said he had to drop out for personal reasons, and his daughter also soon resigned. I was devastated to lose two of the six cast members—especially since I'd already devised the architecture of the script around their stories. I was also very worried about the emotional impact their departure would have on the rest of the group and concerned that others would begin to lose faith and question their own commitment. I needn't have worried. James looked around the room at the remaining cast members and said, "We're such a strong group that we will have to work hard to be welcoming to whoever comes to join us." It was a wonderful reminder to me that groups often hold themselves, and that group leadership can come from anyone. To this day I don't know whether James knows how much strength he gave me by displaying his ongoing faith in the project at that delicate time.

The departure of the two cast members began a rather frenzied process of trying to find new participants. It was the first time in my work that I'd had to replace one-third of the group so late in the process, and it was a daunting task. When we'd met as the original six, I'd had the realization that "by accident" or grace, the makeup of the group revealed a perfect theme: fathers who'd been on the front line during the Troubles and those in the next generation living with the legacy. I hadn't planned it that way, and in fact, had been searching for more adult women for the cast.

But one day I'd taken a fresh look at the group and, as often happens in this work, the problem became the solution. I didn't need to change the composition or balance of the group—the fact that all three men were fathers from republican, loyalist, and security backgrounds was itself compelling, especially when matched with three younger people, one whose father had been assassinated, one whose father had been in prison, and one whose father had been in the security forces. I'd realized that there was an interesting intergenerational dynamic built into the group composition that could serve as the central theme of the production. Since we were focusing primarily on men's stories (other than Victoria's), I decided then that the following year we made sure that the focus was on stories of women in relation to the Troubles. Now I had to find new people to replace the two who had left, while still retaining this core theme.

I have to admit I was resentful of this task. The weight of trying to save the project felt as if it was pushing on my shoulders. So I spent hours watching the clouds and sky from my window. Back in America, clouds are like paintings. One can look up at one, turn away, and see it in the same place in the sky a while later. But here on this emerald isle, clouds seem like films, dancing and dissolving across the sky at almost dizzying speed. I found that they mirrored the changes that were happening in our project. People came and went, reassembling and disassembling. Our group as I knew it dissolved. I was aware that I had a great desire for all to remain static. I wanted everyone to stay. Yet from my window I was finding the movement of the clouds deeply comforting. I decided that the sky would become my teacher. It never clings to clouds.

I went back to my original interviews and invited a few people to join us. We went through a rough period of people trying us out, and us them. We even went fairly far down the road with one man, including me writing his part, before he dropped out. It was disheartening and painful for us all. Eventually, we asked Jon and

Chris to join us. And then later Kieran. I was relieved that they were welcomed with open minds and hearts.

Ecclesiastes

Jon is an impossibly tall man from a republican background who had been active in the IRA during the Troubles. He has a keen sense of history and is now actively involved in peacemaking and education. He already had a professional relationship with Robin and quickly endeared himself to Fionnbharr and Victoria with his outgoing and enthusiastic personality. His personal story, like those of many people in Northern Ireland, was interwoven with the history of Derry and Northern Ireland.

> ...Bloody Sunday. A massacre.
> Thirteen people killed in just eighteen minutes.
> One in front, one behind and one alongside of me.
> Screams, and pure terror.
> People just being slaughtered.
> In Ecclesiastes it says: There's time for everything.
> A time to be born, a time to die.
> A time for war, a time for peace.
> A time to kill, a time to heal.
> Tell me if there's a time to watch a 15-year-old shot, not just once, but shot again when he's on the ground?
> Tell me if there's a time for grandparents, mothers and fathers to bury their children?
> Tell me if there's time to listen to an entire city cry for their dead?
> The funerals. Thirteen coffins.
> It lasted three days—fifty, sixty, seventy thousand people crying.
> Even the heavens cried.
> And the aftermath—empty shoes, fresh flowers and the rain washing blood down the drains.
> It left me wanting to kill. You begin to dehumanize—
> it's not a person—it's the uniform, the number, the name.
> He's just a soldier, just a peeler, just an off-duty cop.
> They all became faceless. They all became the enemy.
> I remember people saying: "It will stop when the first child dies."

It will stop when the first policeman dies, the first soldier,
the first priest, the first woman.
But it didn't stop and it all fueled the anger
and started more waves of retaliation.
I watched young men grow old too quickly and
some not get to grow old at all.
We were in a cycle that seemed impossible to stop.

Jon seemed to fit into the group with ease. Because he knew a lot about Derry and the Troubles, at one rehearsal Victoria suggested that she'd love to go on a tour of the city with him. As soon as she suggested it, I realized it could be very enlightening for us all to go together and to have the three older men show us the places where they remembered being active in pivotal events of the Troubles. The ensuing tour ended up providing the key to Jon and Chris's parts.

The Ripple Effect

We needed to find one more young person, which proved to be more difficult than I'd expected. We had a hard time finding any candidate whose father had been in prison, and wondered if we needed to go in another direction. Early on in the research phase, however, I'd interviewed a fair number of teens, many of whom had been involved in anti-social behavior. They, too, I realized were part of the fabric of Northern Ireland's story and history, and in many ways they represented the ripple effect of the Troubles. In that regard, their stories were also important to tell. Yet most of the teens I'd met weren't emotionally or socially prepared to engage in the Theatre of Witness process. Our coordinator, Nicky, suggested Chris, whom she knew through theatre classes at the University of Ulster, and whom I knew from when he took my Theatre of Witness class at the Playhouse. I asked Nicky to interview him first to vet his story, which I didn't know.

Chris had grown up being influenced by sectarian violence and had engaged in anti-social behavior such as fighting, drugs, and rioting with police as a young teen. He'd grown up without much paternal involvement and had felt disenfranchised and lost. Luckily, he'd had one teacher who'd believed in him and encouraged him to go to university. That experience helped him to turn his life around and he'd become a deeply curious and reflective young man. Chris was a perfect candidate for the production, as he had engaged in behavior similar to that of many of the disenfranchised teens but was now a reliable and stable young man. Eamonn felt that this very story might turn out to be one of the most seminal to the production. He was right. We later heard from many young people who'd seen the show that they particularly resonated with Chris and saw themselves in his story.

> I am the ripple effect
> I don't even know what that means
> I want to get away from this place
> There's nothing here for me
> I'm not interested in hearing anything more about the Troubles
> That's the past
> Their past
> We're the future…
>
> Alcohol, prejudice, fighting,
> Curbs with red, white and blue,
> Curbs with green, white and orange
> A flag in the middle.
> Murals on the electric box
> The IRA with balaclavas and guns
> Where little kids play with their toys
> Lurgan Tonic wine,
> A Buckfast Bottle
> Mayfair lights, burning resin
> Fighting till heads are busted in
> Faces blue and black, teeth knocked out.
> I have a reputation to defend
> Defend my crew
> Getting tense when I see the union jack
> Warm when I see green, white and orange
> I get scared of the prejudice I see in my head
> Who taught me this? Can I make it go away?

You're drunk, you're stoned!
He's stabbed.
Friends steal cars
White van in flames
Burnt out images on TV
Get a buzz, get a high
Bike to Legahory for a 15 lump
Bunk school, play guitar,
Diary entry:
Pills, mushrooms, coke, blow
Roll it and smoke it, snort it, swallow it. Hide the remains
Driving drunk
Driving stoned
Getting caught, do it again.
Tiptoe upstairs
Sleep it off.
Is this all there is?

Empties under the sink
A hole in the wall
Boredom
Hang out with friends, smoke and drink.
Going to school stoned
Taking my tests stoned
What's there to do anyway?
I want to get out of this place

Hear from my dad for the first time when I'm 13.
A Post-it note with his business address:
"Chris—I'd really like to see you—hope you can get back to me."
Pictures of his perfect 2.4 nuclear family.
Fuck.
Picking me up in his Red Landrover
Mum feels intimidated
Playing with the air freshener in his car
Nothing to say
Too much to say
Another world, another life…

One day, at the request of Victoria, Jon led us on a tour of the
Bogside where we went to the place where three of his friends had

been shot during Bloody Sunday.[1] He mourned the fact that youth now hung out in those same places with little awareness about the history that had so shaped them all:

> I walk this city and I see its potential.
> I see the possibilities for peace and justice.
> But when I walk in the Bogside
> I also see the litter and broken bottles.
> I see lost youth sitting on the walls,
> looking for freedom and identity in graffiti, flags and drink.
> They want someone to see them, to know they're there.
> They want to be men, fighters, heroes.
> At age 17 or 18, standing with the disenfranchised
> was our rite of passage.
> It's what gave us voice and turned us into men.
> What rites of passage are left for these young men?
> Do they know they're walking on sacred ground?

While on the tour, Chris took me aside and told me that he used to hang out drinking in graveyards, not thinking of it being hallowed ground for those who died. It was at that moment that I decided we could weave Jon and Chris's stories together, having Jon onstage when Chris talks of an older man walking the Bogside.

> ...I hear the men of this generation talking about growing up
> back then during the war.
> When they talk, there's something so beautiful—
> they had so much passion.
> They had a purpose, something to live for.
> Our generation has passion but we have no purpose.
> Our war is a war on ourselves.
> I walk around the city. I see the alcohol-infused culture
> and I ask myself: "Who is really living?"
> Who is living their own life and who is living
> the remnants of the past?
> When we fight each other, who are we really fighting?
> What is ours? What is theirs?
>
> ...

---

1 January 30, 1972.

An older man walks around the Bogside among the
broken bottles, litter and lost youth sitting on the walls.
They drink and piss on the site where he and his comrades
fought and died, and it breaks his heart.
He shows me the very spot and his voice chokes up.
Those boys were me.
I was once the story of lost youth and disenfranchised dreams.
I pissed on unmarked graves.
I denigrated sacred ground.

Sometimes we don't see things as they are, but as WE are.

I, too, am the ripple effect.
The past, the future, the present, the now.
Another world, another life.

Whatever You Say, Say Nothing

We had our group of six performers and I'd begun scripting their
parts. But as we began to dramatize the scenes, I realized that
without Robin performing live, we were left with only two of
the older generation onstage. Both James and Jon, while strong
performers, had difficulty with line memorization, especially when
combined with movement direction. I needed another body with
a strong physical presence.

I'd seen Kieran when he worked behind the front desk at the
Playhouse and I was struck by his silent, strong, and authoritative
bearing. I didn't know his story but I had a sense that he'd be a
great addition to the cast. He could balance out the energies and
be a powerful physical presence. I tried to entice him to join us by
showing him some previous Theatre of Witness productions on
DVD. He was drawn to the social justice aspect of the work and
wanted to help serve and support the project. He didn't, however,
want to tell his own story. As we talked more, he wasn't sure he
wanted to speak at all in the show. We danced back and forth as
to how he could be most used, and then I remembered the axiom:
"Take the problem and make it the solution." Kieran wanted to be
silent. Silence was a significant theme in the narrative of Northern

Ireland. People had secrets. People were afraid to talk. People were too traumatized to talk. With that insight, I began to weave together some of the images of stories and people I'd heard about and interviewed who weren't in the show.

I remembered going to a very moving evening of testimony with Pauline, during which family members of the disappeared had told their stories. I was haunted by an image of a man I'd interviewed who was dealing with extreme post-traumatic stress disorder and unable to sleep. I thought of those in prison. Some of these images had been stored in my mind but I hadn't known how to use them. Now we could have Kieran represent all those who had been silent, for whatever reason. His part came near the end of the show. He sat still on a chair while, one by one, the performers came and looked at him:

James:

Whatever you say, say nothing.
Whatever you do, don't give anything away.

Jon:

2:00am. He sits at the edge of his bed and shakes. He can't breathe.
The faces of everyone he killed come to bed with him
and infiltrate his dreams.
If he tells anyone about his past he could be shot.
He trusts no one.

Victoria:

He sits at the kitchen table and wishes
they would all leave him alone.
His head is filled again with tangled thoughts like spaghetti.
He remembers when he threw his heart into the ring and gave his
whole life for the freedom struggle.
But now he doesn't like the way things are going.
He knows he should speak out, or make himself known.
But he no longer believes in violent struggle
and he doesn't want to put his family at risk.
So he sits at the kitchen table and stares at the wall.

Fionnbharr:

She sits and waits at the table.
Her hands, smoothing the tablecloth.
No one's heard from him for over 14 years.
She knows in her head that he was done by one of his own.
But her heart isn't ready to believe.
She wants justice.
She wants answers.
She wants once more to hear his voice.
But no one says anything. No one gives anything away.
She sits and waits for her disappeared son.

Fionnbharr almost always sobbed his way through these last words. He was talking about a mother and her disappeared son, yet it was his own story of yearning for answers and justice on behalf of his murdered father that fueled his tears. It was one of the most touching parts of the production for me—a moment where stories interlinked, and the pain of one person's struggle was held and felt by someone else. It felt like he was carrying the pain of all those in Northern Ireland.

But Fionnbharr almost always came to these words already in tears. During his part, just before this, he usually cried onstage with his head resting on his drum, listening to his own story on film. I'd known early on that it would be too traumatizing to have him recite his part over and over each night, so I'd thought of having his part shown on film while he drummed in front of it onstage. Music was his medicine and gave him a way to express his pain without words. I thought drumming would bring him back to his strength and center. But when we tried this, it became clear that his recorded voice and the sound of the drums fought each other onstage. So he drummed before the film, cried during it, and drummed again at the end.

I worried about Fionnbharr, as did our team and many in the audience. One person wrote on her audience reflection that she was afraid that we were re-traumatizing him. But from the beginning, I trusted his own sense of agency. He was a strong and very independent young man who was clear about what he wanted to do. I, as well as counselors we'd teamed with, continued to check in with him and also to observe his behavior. Over the course of the rehearsals and performances, Fionnbharr seemed to get more and more comfortable with the other cast members, including Robin and James, both of whom were the "perceived enemy," and people he had been wary of connecting with at the beginning. Each smoking break, we'd see Fionnbharr, a young man from a staunch republican background, and James, an older former loyalist paramilitary, outside, rolling their cigarettes together. They became buddies, and if there had been a thing called the "smoking team," they were the co-leaders, following each other out the door, spending hours and hours together over the time of the project. Fionnbharr played the young James in James's part—actually stepping into his history and skin. He did it with integrity and commitment.

The day that Robin brought in his RUC uniform, Fionnbharr, who believed his father had been killed by RUC collusion, kept his head down, never looking at either Robin or the uniform. We could see the courage that it took for him to wrestle to overcome his fears and prejudice. We all knew it was a big deal for him to be in a room with a member of the police. But Robin was very understanding and respectful of Fionnbharr's feelings. He took things slowly and spoke about understanding that people had many intense feelings about the police. Things softened between them. By opening night, they spent the day texting each other about an elaborate practical joke the two of them decided to play on me. I got to the theatre, and Robin said, "I assume by now you know that Fionnbharr was arrested last night? I'm going to leave now and try to get him out of jail." I freaked. We had about two hours before the show started and I couldn't imagine how we could do it without him. I ran around the theatre in a complete dither, furious at Fionnbharr for getting himself in trouble with the law just before the première. Robin let me go on in that state for about 15 minutes before he and Fionnbharr appeared together and let me in on the joke. Later, Robin said that the joke had been Fionnbharr's idea, and the fact that he had wanted Robin in on it was a real sign of the relationship they'd developed.

Fionnbharr, however, continued to cry each time he saw his film being played. I trusted my sense that this was all part of the natural grieving process, but to be sure I wanted to a have a mental health assessment with some outside professionals. To that end, I invited two different therapists to come in and observe. Each said they felt he was working through his grieving process. He happened to be doing it publicly, but they felt he was moving through it and not re-traumatizing himself. After the first performance, I held him, as tears kept coming. To find out whether performing had been too much emotionally for him, I asked what he wanted to do the next night. "Come back and perform again." To many of us, it looked unbearable, but I trusted Fionnbharr's own clarity that this was something he wanted to do. He invited many of his friends and family to come see the show as it toured. I think it was his way of making sure they knew his story as well as his grief. He later said that doing the project was the best therapy he ever had, that we hadn't tried to "fix him," we'd just let him be. That statement confirmed my strong belief that it is in meeting and accepting the pain and suffering rather than trying to change it that real healing can begin.

I also believe that Fionnbharr played a very important role for the audience. During Jon's part about Bloody Sunday, there was a moment when Fionnbharr, playing a gunshot victim, totally collapsed into Kieran's arms, almost like a baby or a Christ-like image. The movement had come organically from directions I'd given in a rehearsal, but I'd never imagined that particular position or Fionnbharr's complete surrender. Each time Kieran held and rocked him, I think his vulnerability stirred compassion and deep empathy for so many who saw it. He became the emotional lightning rod and invited us all to touch that place of suffering within ourselves—that place where true compassion lies.

The Audience Bears Witness

We were all quite nervous to see how *We Carried Your Secrets* would be received. While some powerful plays have been produced about the Troubles, to our knowledge there were few that were in the Theatre of Witness form, performed by people from a variety of backgrounds coming together to share their own personal stories of their involvement with the Troubles. And while Northern Ireland hosts transformational peace and reconciliation programs that bring ex-combatants from republican, loyalist, and security force groups together with victims, that work is primarily done behind closed doors in very safe private and confidential settings. We were bringing what is often done in private out to a public setting in the form of theatre. Our intention was for audiences to bear witness to the stories of trauma and transformation, humanize the perceived enemy, and be moved and inspired to cross the cultural divide. We hoped the performances would prove to be safe events for the performers as well as for audience members.

Following each performance, we had a post-performance discussion during which audience members could give feedback and ask questions. It was at one of the first of these audience discussions that Kathleen Gillespie raised her hand to speak. Kathleen, the widow of Patsy Gillespie, had come to the show prepared, knowing that Robin would be talking about the horrific bomb explosion at Coshquin that had killed her husband. We were all concerned that she not be re-traumatized by the description of the bomb scene, and that she'd feel that we'd honored the memory of her husband. It was a delicate situation, and we were all greatly moved when she spoke about the power of the show and thanked us.

When the discussion was over, she asked me if I would be willing to give her phone number to Robin. She wanted to ask him questions about the bomb scene that had been haunting her since Patsy's death. Robin, who'd been on the body recovery team at Coshquin, knew as much as anyone could know about some of the graphic facts of his death. Kathleen had been dealing for years with nightmares about what was in his coffin. She wanted to know the truth. Generously, Robin agreed to meet with her and she later told me that their meeting had helped give her the closure she'd been so deeply seeking. When I spoke with Robin, he reported feeling humbled and gratified that he'd been able to help in some small way. It was one of the most powerful and positive outcomes to come out of *We Carried Your Secrets*.

At each performance, we also handed out reflection sheets for audience members to write their feelings and thoughts. We received hundreds, many with responses similar to these:

> This was amazing. I'm shaking. Thank you. Thank you. Thank you for sharing your stories with us. For being part of this program. For giving so much of yourself to us and for letting me see myself in you. You are brave and your bravery is what will bring us to a new reality in Northern Ireland... Thank you just seems not close enough.

> Tell the truth it will release you. This was for me a great night. I hope there will be more. I think this will go far to heal our people. We are much the same. We all hurt.

> Tonight I came here with views on things I thought I understood, I made judgments on things I thought I understood, but tonight I realized I had no idea about things except through a sort of narrow, clinical, microscopic tunnel vision based on facts and figures and dates in subjective history. Tonight these judgments have been shattered and I have been left not knowing how I feel, but I hope that now I can look at things in the future with new eyes based on hope and forgiveness and new awareness. Thank you.

> This was like open-heart surgery on the city of Derry.

> Powerful. Raw. Brave... How can any of [us] writers create characters or purport to speak for the survivors when you speak so eloquently for yourselves?

> I think it was the most profoundly moving experience I've ever had in the theatre, or anywhere else really for that matter. You've made me re-evaluate almost everything that I felt about the past and my political convictions. I feel utterly and completely transformed from having seen the performance. I think this is germinating more goodwill and genuine

reconciliation through truth as opposed to recrimination through truth that we have too much of in this place.

I don't think that the performers were prepared for the extraordinarily positive reactions they received. They were thanked, hugged, and given much appreciation and gratitude. There were standing ovations at almost all of the shows, and often the performers were flooded with well-wishers wanting to connect on a personal level. We performed 14 times throughout the North and across the border, and as the performers got more and more comfortable, they seemed to grow in confidence and wisdom. I think for most of them it didn't take many performances before they truly understood that they were putting themselves through the emotion of their stories not for themselves, but for those in the audience who received solace, hope, and inspiration from them.

CHAPTER 14

Your People are My People

Unheard Women's Stories—
Northern Ireland

After focusing primarily on men's stories of the Troubles in *We Carried Your Secrets*, I longed to be immersed in what I saw as the sacred feminine. It's what initially drew me to the island of Ireland and I wanted to explore its qualities and influence. For me, the sacred feminine is an ethereal and spacious energy of love. It's a healing power that serves as a potent antidote to the dark and thick violence of war and social upheaval. I wanted to find it in imagery, music, scene design, and movement. I wanted to see what would emerge if we permeated the stories of women deeply affected by violence with beauty, delicacy, and tenderness. I wondered if the very medicine for this troubled island was already deeply embedded in its land, culture, music, and mythology. I didn't yet know how we'd do this. I just knew where I was drawn.

I had many questions about the roles and feelings of women who had lived through the Troubles. How were mothers, wives, and daughters affected by the involvement of their loved ones? How did women combatants differ from their male counterparts? How did women hold their families together? How were women living with familial violence, depression, alcoholism, abuse, and poverty? What were the effects on them of the anti-social behavior of youth and the suicide epidemic? What role did women play in peacebuilding? What were women's dreams? Could we create a community of women that would in itself be a model of healing?

Water

After the cast of six performers had been chosen, again from republican, loyalist, and security force backgrounds, we had a two-day residential, during which everyone shared their story and we did experiential exercises that helped the group to bond and create community. One of my goals for our time together was to explore the realm of beauty. I asked the women to bring items from their homes that we would use to decorate the communal space. For our last exercise together during the residential, I decided to experiment with water imagery, hoping it might prove to be a fertile field of improvisation. I brought in some empty buckets,

bowls, cups, and glasses, and a large container of water. I first led
the group in a ritual of offering libations, adapted from the African
tradition of pouring liquid to bless the earth and offer gratitude
and blessing to the ancestors. I had each woman fill her cup from
the communal water, walk to the front, and finish the stem of the
sentence "In honor of…" or "In gratitude for…," before pouring
the water into a second communal vessel. We played background
music and I let the ritual go on for a good 15 minutes before
leading them into a large circle to simultaneously pour their water
and create a group blessing. I was pleased that, new and strange as
this ritual was for the women, they brought themselves fully into
the spirit of the moment.

From there, I invited them to improvise with the water
elements, relating to each other as they experimented. I watched
and made suggestions as they tenderly washed each other's faces
and feet, gently held glasses for one another to drink, washed
each other's hair, played in delight, and created a fountain of
water being poured from glass to bowl to glass. It mesmerized me,
and that exercise brought them together as a group and soothed
some of the tension over political differences that had come up
in discussion. The water seemed to create a sense of flow and
universality. The pouring became its own dance, and the sounds
of water splashing became a soothing musical accompaniment. I
knew then that we wouldn't have to rely on the women's abilities
to dance or move onstage—the water would do it for us.

When we broke to talk about what the experience had been
like, words like "healing," "cleansing," "beautiful," and "loving"
were expressed. I shared with them my idea to incorporate water
as a central image for the show, and they were enthused. I knew
it could provide thematic connective tissue, a sense of movement,
a balm for the difficult and dark stories, and a ritual element that
would bind them together as a group. This opened an artistic
pathway for me and I felt as though, together, we would be able
to find fresh and meaningful images to enhance their stories. I
knew then also that this new production wouldn't feel only like a
continuation of *We Carried Your Secrets*. It would have its own flavor.

Letters from Afar

The first woman to join our cast was Kathleen Gillespie. I had first met her at a post-performance discussion for *We Carried Your Secrets.* A strong and forthright woman, she congratulated us on the performance, and, responding to my announcement about a new project, let me know that she'd love to be a participant in this new production. I was elated and not a little daunted, because Kathleen is a confident and born leader, and the story of her husband Patsy's murder is one of the most seminal of the Northern Ireland Troubles. There could be no holding back. But I also knew that her involvement meant that we had a strong backbone from the very beginning.

I interviewed Kathleen numerous times and was overwhelmed by the magnitude of her story—it was epic in proportion and deeply tragic. It was an interviewer's dream to meet with her, as she was confident in her recounting, shared many rich details, and wasn't afraid to let herself feel the fullness of her emotions. I was moved to tears by her and knew that the audience would be also. But if anything, I was afraid that her story could easily overpower those of the other women, and I had to make sure that her strength wouldn't diminish anyone in the group. I needn't have worried, as Kathleen is a deeply empathic woman who drew the other women into her love and care. I think that her strength actually inspired the other women to grow more fully into their own. For all of those qualities, she was a dream to work with.

The other concern I had is that many people in Northern Ireland knew of the assassination of Patsy Gillespie from extensive media coverage over the years, and may have felt that they already knew her story. But the more I listened to Kathleen, the more I realized that people didn't know the story from her perspective of being a wife, mother, and woman. And in fact, the very reason we were making *I Once Knew a Girl* was to illuminate the unheard stories of women who'd been affected by the Troubles equally with men. People also might not have known Kathleen's story about working through her pain and loss by becoming a peacemaker, a powerful force in the healing of Northern Ireland.

Before I had begun writing her script, Kathleen shared some of the hundreds of letters she'd saved from people all over the world after Patsy's death. They ranged from eloquent condolences from a 17-year-old boy, to priests, to those who had read about it from abroad, and to those who knew the family intimately. I knew immediately that they could be a powerful thread in her story. I sifted through them, choosing some that could be read by the other performers during her part. Her piece began with the whole cast sitting on a staircase where, one by one, each performer read from a letter. The look on Kathleen's face when she heard the women read was one of deep sadness and reverie.

Dear Mrs. Gillespie and family:

I have never written to anyone before like this but I wanted to let you know that there are people world wide who feel for you and focus their love on you. Having seen the horror of what the IRA have done, we wish to send you our condolences and wishes. Mr. Gillespie has not died in vain—one day there will be peace. Our father's family was killed in the Treblinka concentration camp in 1934.

A sympathizer—Australia

Dear Kathleen:

Please accept my heartfelt sympathy at your time of great loss. No words can express how my heart feels for you, as my husband was murdered this year in front of our two young sons aged eight and five. So like yourself and your three children, our three children and myself are totally devastated and don't know how to carry on. I have found that people on both sides of the community really do care and, like you and me, cannot understand why men like Patsy and my husband, who are innocent family men, end up as victims. There are so many questions and no answers.

Northern Ireland...

From there, Kathleen began her story with her dream of growing up one day to become a wife and mother. She spoke about meeting Patsy at 16, marrying at 20, bearing two sons and then finally, at great physical risk to herself, giving birth to a daughter for Patsy. Her dreams had all come true. Patsy, who was Catholic, had nothing to do with the Troubles, but due to the violence on the street, he lost his fruit and vegetable stand and went to work on the army base. There had been warnings in the paper from paramilitaries about working on the base, but Patsy needed to support his family.

> The first trouble was in 1986 when our house was taken over
> by the IRA. Patsy was forced to drive our car to the army base
> loaded down with 200 pounds of explosives.
> That time he was able to jump out
> and shout that the car was loaded.
> They did a controlled explosion and he got home around 6 am.
> After that, the Ministry of Defence said they'd move us
> anywhere we wanted, but Patsy was adamant.
> "No one will put me out of my home."
> We thought that lightning couldn't strike twice. But it's not true.
> Four years later they eventually succeeded in killing Patsy.

> …This time they chained Patsy to a van, loaded it with
> 1000 pounds of explosives, made him drive to the army checkpoint
> and then detonated it remotely.
> Five army soldiers as well as Patsy were blown up in the explosion…
> The worst for me is that I think that from midnight on,
> Patsy knew that he was going to die.
> They couldn't let him go, knowing they could be recognized,
> and they would have had to take their masks off to cross the border.

> I think that Patsy had four hours knowing that he was going
> to be murdered, wondering how they were gonna kill him.
> It must have been hell for him.
> But what must have been the worst for him was knowing
> he would never see his family again.

> But what must have been the worst for him was knowing he would
> never see his family again.

Kathleen described the horror of having to tell her eldest son Patrick on the phone that his father had been murdered. He screamed: "*I'll kill those Bastards.*"

I wanted to identify the body at the mortuary but they said
"I'm sorry Mrs. Gillespie, the coffin is closed."
There was nothing to identify. No final proof of his death.
So until the time of the inquest,
a part of me still thought that Patsy
was in hiding somewhere and that eventually he would phone
for me and send me tickets to bring the wains to wherever he was.
Common sense told me he was dead, but I was living in constant
preparations to move at a minute's notice.

About a month after his death, there was a howling wind
and lashing rain. The branches of the rose bush in front
of my bedroom window were scratching against the glass.
I couldn't sleep. I thought it was Patsy trying to get in through
the window. So at 3:00 am I put a coat on, went out
and cut the rose bush down to the roots.

At the inquest they talked about the numbered body bags.
I realized that none of them knew what was in the coffin.
I had terrible nightmares about him being put together wrong.
I couldn't sleep with the nightmares.
One night I finally propped myself up with me book and thought,
"I'm terrified to go to sleep."
And the next thing, I looked down at the door, and
Patsy was standing at the door.
Now, I wasn't asleep. I was propped up. I had me book in me hand.
I had my glasses on.
I looked at the door and Patsy was standing there
with his gray cardigan that he'd been wearing
when he was taken away.
He said "Look at me girl, I'm OK. Go to sleep now."
And that was that.
I went to a healing service in the church that Sunday evening,
and the priest preached, "On the last day when we all arise perfect."
And I thought, this is for me.
Final proof that Patsy was OK wherever he was.

It felt very important to me to have Kathleen include the story of
Patsy's presence in the bedroom following his death. It felt like
a doorway to the spirit world that I'd hoped so much to evoke.
Onstage, we projected a slide of a beautiful rose bush behind

Kathleen while she spoke. When the image was turned off, it was as if Patsy, too, had just disappeared.

Kathleen's part continued with her describing the early days of grief and how proud she is that none of her children joined paramilitary organizations to avenge their father's death. The audience then learns about her peace work, the blessing wrought from the wound of grief.

> What actually brought me back to sanity was that I
> became involved in a peace and reconciliation program.
> I remember the first time it was suggested that I meet with
> ex-combatants, I got dreadful flashbacks.
> The very thought of confronting an ex-IRA man or
> somebody like that—to even look at them,
> never mind talk to them—was horrific. I just panicked.
> I actually got up and ran out of the room.
>
> But then I began to say to myself, "If I'm one of the people who
> wants peace, and I am, then I need to be prepared to meet
> these people, mix with them, talk to them, and hear their stories
> and what they have to say.
> And if I'm not prepared to do this,
> how can I expect other people in Northern Ireland
> to do this work?"
> So I've been meeting with ex-paramilitaries for the past 15 years.
> Some of them have even become friends.
> I confront and challenge them to meet up with the
> people they injured. In terms of justice, things are still up in the air.
> Five men were arrested for the crime, but were let go after a
> couple of months because of insufficient evidence.
> Some even got compensation for wrongful imprisonment...
> Twenty years have passed, and I continue my work with
> ex-combatants and I'm still active in pursuing the case for justice.
> I won't give up.
> My family has grown, and I'm now the grandmother
> of four beautiful babies.
> My eldest son Patrick wears his father's wedding ring...
> I feel Patsy on my shoulder guiding special people to me,
> to help and guide me through.
> He is always with me giving me strength.

> When I was picking Patsy's headstone, I wanted to write:
> "Murdered by the IRA" on it.
> But instead I had them engrave the words:
> "Lord, let him be an instrument of thy peace."
> I pray he did not die in vain.

For me, this change from "Murdered by the IRA" to "Lord, let him be an instrument of thy peace" was as powerful a turnaround of peace as I could imagine.

Dreams of a Girl

Whenever I interview potential participants for a Theatre of Witness production, I almost always ask them about the dreams they had for themselves when they were young. Who did they imagine they'd be? What did they most want for themselves? Sometimes I ask what the familial expectations for them had been and how they had reacted to them. I was surprised, when interviewing women for *I Once Knew a Girl*, at how many of them had dreamed of becoming a wife and mother. Coming of age in the 1960s in America, so many of us had dreamed of careers. I had always wanted to get married and have children, but I couldn't have imagined living a life like my mother's where, after marriage, she stayed home to take care of four children. I had always assumed that I'd be a professional dancer, teacher, or choreographer. But here in Northern Ireland, I had to recalibrate my thinking. The abundant options that had been available to me and my cohorts in white, upper middle-class America were very different from the limited ones available for women in Northern Ireland who lived through the violence of the Troubles. The influences of church and family were all-prevailing, as were poverty and the cultural expectations for women. Feminism hadn't yet infiltrated mainstream society in Ireland as it had for the past 40 years in the United States, and for many of the women I interviewed, the promise of motherhood was a powerful dream of fulfillment. I found myself rethinking my own attitudes and assumptions about the roles of women and wondered about the price my own children had paid for my expansive dreams.

When I was a child, some of my most comforting times were when I was snuggled next to our babysitter, Mrs. Macdonald, as she'd sing our favorite song, "Que sera sera" ("Whatever will be will be"). The song seemed to reflect the questions of my pre-teen, pre-feminist self, when I wondered how my life would turn out and who I'd become.

I'd completely forgotten about that song, until an ocean away, 50 years later, Maria (one of the performers) brought it up during an interview. It had been a deeply important song in her childhood as well, and she even had a recording of herself singing it as a little girl. When she sang it for me, I felt the ocean dissolve and time collapse. There was something about those young girl questions that was universal. Maria later sang it to the whole group, and the song became almost like a talisman. We found ourselves singing it together as part of an ending ritual for all of our meetings.

Concurrently, as part of my initial research, I met with one of Northern Ireland's dynamic MLAs,[1] Dawn Purvis. I'd heard her give an inspiring talk and knew that she had her pulse on women's issues. At our meeting, she spoke about her own life growing up poor in South Belfast during the Troubles. She talked about having once been just like some of the women she now served—women who have a poverty of aspiration. She told me that she often began speeches with the phrase "I once knew a girl." She'd follow that phrase with descriptions of a girl wearing pajama bottoms to the shops in the afternoon, watching soaps on TV, and having few dreams of possibility. That girl, her younger self, was someone who never could have imagined the educated and highly professional woman that Dawn later became. Moved by her story, I asked if she'd be willing to be a performer. But in her political role as an MLA at that time, it was impossible. So instead, I borrowed her phrase, which we used as the title and central theme of the show.

---

1 Member of Legislative Assembly, Northern Ireland.

Combining the theme of "I once knew a girl" and the song "Que sera sera," I decided to create a prologue for the production performed by a teenage girl on the cusp of womanhood. Slowly and dreamily, the girl entered, looking out towards the horizon. She climbed the stairs, sat on top, and lazily circled her foot in the imaginary water as she sang the verse from the song. The girl, who never spoke throughout the production, represented the younger self of all the women. Following the scene of the girl imagining her future, the women's stories unfolded, contrasting their youthful dreams with the realities of who they'd become after living through war. That became one of the central threads of the show. Catherine's story followed.

An Ordinary Girl

I was an ordinary little girl
growing up off the Shankill Road in the 1960s.
I dreamed of getting married and one day living in my own house.
I decorated that house in my mind for years.
Outside it was going to have an old-fashioned street lamp and pump painted black with gold trim.
Inside, three bedrooms, a real leather suite and an indoor toilet.
It would have a garden out back with slides and swings for the children to play.
I was an ordinary girl, dreaming ordinary dreams,
but you could say my teenage years got taken away by the Troubles.

The first story in the performance was Catherine's. It seemed a gentle way to introduce the themes of family and community. It also established some of the questions that underpinned the show: What happens when the abnormal becomes normalized during times of war, conflict, and post-conflict? What does "ordinary" mean during extraordinary times? How will the history of a conflict seem different through the eyes and ears of everyday people, rather than through the lens of its perceived heroes and warriors—mostly men? A final question emerged after hearing so often from the women I interviewed that they believed their story wasn't special or worthy of being told: How does the prevalence of violence, abuse, and conflict in times like the Troubles cause people to minimize their own pain and suffering? I wanted this production to engage these questions through personal stories of women from varied backgrounds. They had each experienced the years of conflict differently, but I was interested in what they held in common.

Catherine and I first met at the community center near her home, where she'd been instrumental in setting up educational and violence prevention programs for loyalist women and youth. I was very taken with her the first time we met. She has a deep yet soft speaking voice, and is clearly a strong woman. She walks with a limp since contracting polio as a young girl, yet she exudes an inner authority and humor that make it impossible for anyone to look at her physical disability with pity. I was moved by her devotion to her community. She grew up close to where one of the other performers, Therese, had once lived on the Falls Road—a highly republican area. Their communities had been, and still are, to some extent, in conflict. The stories of women from working-class Protestant loyalist areas are in some ways the least heard in Northern Ireland, and I knew that Catherine would be a powerful voice for them.

> It all started one night with the sound of our
> windows being shattered.
> Men were in an open lorry going down our street trying to
> smash as many doors and windows as they could.
> Then it became nightly... Our street was under siege.
> The fathers went off to work during the day and then came back
> and guarded the corners at night.
> They became known as the vigilantes.
> The mothers were out every morning sweeping up the debris,
> making tea, sandwiches and big pots of soup.
>
> They took up collections for petrol, even siphoning it from cars
> at night to make bombs in the vacant houses.
> Finally, guns were brought in
> and the men barricaded every entrance to the street.
> They did it in shifts, staying up all night, protecting our homes.

The next thing all of a sudden the British Army was on our streets.
At first I remember the women cheering them.
They were welcomed in both areas.
But then both the army and police came under attack…
You become a prisoner in your own home.
One by one, my friends and their families started emigrating;
I can remember going down to the boat, to see them off.
You know, me crying and them crying and it just broke my heart.
The ones that went to Australia I've never, ever seen them again.
But I never, ever forgot them.

In Catherine's part I had attempted to paint a picture of the everyday life in the streets during the Troubles from the perspective of a young girl from a loyalist community. While Catherine narrated her story, the rest of the women silently created a series of vignettes on the main part of the stage, metaphorically walking in her shoes and story.

…Our street took the brunt of it when our street lamps got smashed and the pavements were ripped up to have something to throw at the police.
It was mayhem.
A group of women began to stand at the interface to stop the kids from congregating and many riots were prevented.
With the help of a local councilor we became the Woodvale and Cambria Youth and Community Group.
We were 60 strong and we accomplished a lot, giving kids a safe place to be and grow. I feel as though I found my voice there, offering something to the youth.
…I think back to the dreams I had as a little girl growing up.
I did marry, and bought my first house,
but it was a wee two-up two-down like I'd come from.
No black and gold street lamp or indoor toilet,
but I did that outside one up with paper and paint,
and made it as modern as I could. I was proud of that wee house.
As a young girl, I hadn't yet lived enough to know
the power of dreams.
The dream of letting go of bitterness.
The dream of raising three children and two grandchildren, with none of them involved in organizations.

The dream of being proud to be a woman, mother and grandmother.
I'm proud of what I've done with my wee life.
Now I don't dream for myself.
I dream for my children and grandchildren.
And for your children and grandchildren too.

Allying with Beauty

Therese is gentle and delicate. That's what struck me about her at our first meeting around a kitchen table in a family support center in Derry. I was there to introduce myself to a small group of women, to see if they'd be interested in meeting with me a few times to talk about their lives related to abuse, addiction, depression, and parenting. I hoped maybe one or two of them might end up being performers in the new project. I'd only just begun my introduction when my eyes rested upon a diminutive and beautiful woman who intrigued me with her silent demeanor. Some inexplicable connection was forged in the instant that our eyes met. Intuition guided me to suggest that I'd be available to meet individually first, in case any of the women would prefer that, before meeting with the group. Therese, who had always been too scared to talk in group therapy, immediately took me up on my offer and our relationship grew from there.

When we met, I was struck by two very different things. The first was the absolute horrific violence, abuse, and poverty Therese had endured. I've rarely met anyone who has endured more trauma in her life. But somehow, her inner strength and love of beauty hadn't been dampened. For all the dark and terrible things that had happened to her, there was a light that emanated from her eyes and a grace and delicateness in her spirit. She seemed like a tender new flower, waiting to bloom.

Therese's story encompassed both familial violence as well as the tragedy of the Troubles:

One July morning, I remember Daddy telling us that
trouble was starting and we should stay away from the bonfires.
He went off to work and Mummy was in the kitchen
boiling nappies. "Don't go!"

Then we heard shootings.
That night there were gangs outside the house.
"We know you're in there hiding in the dark, you Feinians.
We're not stupid!"

Mummy told us, "I'm going to get Granda.
If I'm not back in ten minutes, you'll know I've been shot."
We were all terrified, crying and squealing.
Another time Daddy came in and said
he'd been told that we were being put out.
The front door was open and I saw a big gun facing the house.
Mummy ran into the street shouting,
"You were supposed to be our friends, now you're putting us out?"
The car was too small for our things.
The only thing Mummy lifted was the sewing machine.
Mummy had no coat. We went to Daddy's sisters,
my aunt gave her a coat, but they said there was no room for us.
We ended up in the Holy Child School where it seemed like there
were thousands of other families.
I stuck to my Mummy like glue. I was quiet,
but I was always listening. I still always listen.
My aunt tried to go back into our house the next day,
but it was cordoned off.
The soldiers told her that there was nothing left to it.
We saw them taking the furniture, light it on fire
and dance around it while it burned.
The soldiers told us,
"There's another family living in the house now."
We were like refugees. No one wanted to take us in…

Therese's family was forced out of many homes and her schooling
was interrupted so often that she eventually stopped going.
Consequently, she didn't learn to read until she was in her
thirties. While her outer world had been violated so terribly with
sectarianism, her innermost world was also shattered by sexual
abuse. She kept it secret, as most children do, and retreated into
her make-believe world.

When Therese told me about her love of angels and fairytales
I was captivated by her rich imaginative life that was like a secret

garden where she retreated when she had to disassociate from the ugliness of violence. Coupled with her love of dance and gymnastics, it was clear that no one had been able to damage her innate beauty. I trusted that strength and beauty and actively chose to ally with it, rather than with the scars of her wounds. I invited her to come into the dance studio, where I put music on and directed her in some movement improvisations. While she didn't have much technical training, her elegance and ability to enter into a deep, almost trancelike state of dance encouraged me to further explore this movement as a way for her to perform, as well as a safe landing pad for her as she accessed the stories of violation. I knew right away that I wanted to use film to highlight some of her imagery, and possibly to show close-ups of her dancing.

> The worst thing that happened to me then was at
> my Grannie's house. My cousin took me there
> and there was nobody else at home.
> I said, "I want to go home!"
> But he said, "No—we'll go soon. We'll play a wee game
> and we'll play music or hide and seek."
> He went upstairs to hide.
> I thought I could get out the door, but I couldn't reach the latch
> and I was trying to get the latch off the door and
> I heard him calling me,
> "If you don't come and get me, you'll never go home!"
> There was a big velvet curtain that hung on the stairs.
> I knew that once I passed the curtain and went up the stairs...
> Each stair was like forever.
> I just put my hand on the handle of the door
> and that's where he brought me.
> I kept closing my eyes and saying, "I want to go home,
> I want to go home!"
> And he said I could go home
> after he did what he wanted to do to me.
> And then he told me not to tell anybody.
> Something bad was happening. Something so dark and scary.
> I went into the pretend world where I am always safe.
> The world of fairytales and angels where I can be anybody I want.
> Like the Little Mermaid and Cinderella.

I love those beautiful dresses.
I love dolls, imaginary antique houses that smell of clean wood
and fairies and angels.
I love their wee wings.
In my dreams I can put my arms out and just rise up into the air.
I'm dancing, flying free…

Onstage, Therese mounted a white staircase, while behind her a film was projected of a foreboding flight of wooden steps. When she reached the top of the staircase, Therese closed her eyes: "Something bad was happening. Something so dark and scary." The stair images then dissolved into those of porcelain angels as she continued with her eyes closed: "I went into the pretend world where I am always safe. The world of fairytales and angels where I can be anybody I want." We observed her inner world being replicated on film. The ugliness of sexual violation contrasted with the calm beauty of the angels. It was a poignant and stark vision of her method of keeping her spirit intact.

The process of rehearsing with Therese continually surprised me. At the beginning, when she first told her story about the abuse, sometimes she'd feel sick and we'd have to stop. But as we peppered the rehearsals with the imagery of angels and dancing, she was able to tolerate talking about additional details of those dark experiences. Therese had often been accused by family members and even by some therapists of not living in the "real world." They wanted her to "grow up." I felt, however, that her imagination was the key to her healing. She just had not had enough safe and appropriate expressive outlets for her creative impulses. Once she was given an opportunity to dance to music she loved, to talk in detail about her angels, and to be appreciated by our group for her grace and gentleness, she began to thrive. Then the most remarkable thing happened. She was the first one of the performers to memorize her part. Because Therese hadn't learned to read until she was an adult, she had been very reticent to read any of it out loud to our group. She also had a lot of self-doubt about her ability to memorize her lines. Her success at it was in direct contrast to her negative beliefs about herself, and the group was vociferous in reminding her of her gifts.

We all watched Therese grow in confidence and bloom onstage in rehearsals. I wanted the ending of her part to reflect strength, so I took a few more liberties in the writing than I usually do. I wrote the following ending part more from my sense of her story and the trajectory I wanted to offer her, rather than directly from her words. I wanted her to name her own growth and strength. I chose to put it in a poetic form because I knew she loved poetry. When she read it the first time, she loved it and it soon became her favorite part. This was the real medicine:

> I once knew a girl who lost herself…
> I once knew a girl whose marriage was haunted by her history of sexual abuse.
> Who suffered depression and isolation and couldn't tell why.
> Who divorced, and then met a man who beat and abused her.
> Whose daughter watched while he tortured her with violence; verbal, physical and more.
>
> I once knew a girl who became silent and ashamed.
> Who believed the abuse and thought herself stupid.
> Who never spoke up, and lived in fear.
> Who lost her will to live and was abandoned by hope.
> But I once knew a girl who grew into her strength.
> Who learned to say NO, and claimed back her own life.
> Who never stopped imagining even when her world was dark.
> Who got help and support and found she wasn't alone.
> I am that girl. Therese Parker McCann.
> A woman of strength.

It took a long while for Therese to perform that last line with full authority. She rehearsed it over and over, trying to uncover her authentic, embodied strength, with much support and direction from me. When she was finally able to say it with full vocal power, it was viscerally thrilling for all of us. She grew into her strength and became a model for so many in the audience who saw their own story reflected in hers. For me, she was the embodiment of beauty and wounding—a personified glimpse into the heart of Northern Ireland.

Extraordinary Circumstances

When I began recruiting performers for *I Once Knew a Girl*, I was aware that it might be hard to find a female ex-combatant who was willing to share her story publicly. I also knew that, unlike the many ex-combatant groups populated by men, women who had been active in paramilitary groups during the Troubles probably were then, and remain now, more hidden in society. I was afraid that it would be almost impossible to find a suitable candidate.

I cast the net wide, and spoke with male ex-combatants with whom I already had connections. One of them knew Anne well, and felt that Theatre of Witness would give her a much needed opportunity to finally process the effects of those heady years of combat. He knew of her current emotional distress and felt that some of it was due to all the untold stories and emotions she'd bottled up for years.

During our initial individual interviews, Anne cried almost constantly. It was as if a spigot had gotten turned on and there was no off switch. She cried so much that it took me a while to discern whether she was stable enough to participate in the process. I checked back with the man who had recommended her and he expressed great confidence in her inner strength. He believed that her tears were just an emotional release and that the project would be a great healing for her. He also believed that she'd be a powerful performer. As I spent more time with Anne, her upset slowly lessened and I began to see her strength and humor seeping through. I started to trust that she would thrive in our creative process and that she had a lot to offer the project.

Probably the most important factor for me in deciding to choose Anne for the cast was that she no longer believed in violence as the method for fighting for freedom. She understood the horrific impact the war had had on so many lives and she felt remorse for her own younger involvement. I never pretend that

Theatre of Witness is a form that presents all views. For me, the ultimate purpose of the work is that it be a model for peace. Like my previous work with prisoners, former soldiers, and perpetrators, I always look for performers who have done the deep work of transformation from hatred and violence to understanding and peace. The courage to confront one's most deeply held beliefs, to take accountability for one's actions and to grieve for the pain one has caused, is the very medicine at the center of this work.

When I first interviewed Anne, before we even got into the content of her story, I prepared her for the fact that Kathleen Gillespie was going to be part of the cast. Like most people in Northern Ireland, Anne knew that Kathleen was the widow of Patsy Gillespie who had been so brutally murdered by the IRA. She knew that sharing her story of being an IRA combatant with one of Northern Ireland's most well-known victims would be extraordinarily painful. But she was courageous and drawn to the possibility of great healing that their working together might engender.

I never would have attempted to bring these two women together if I hadn't also known that Kathleen had already done a lot of behind-closed-doors peace and reconciliation work with ex-combatants. She had a large capacity for understanding and she had already demonstrated the ability to be empathic towards ex-combatants. I knew it would probably be difficult for both women, but I also firmly believed that it would turn out positively.

When the full group finally met for the first time, as with all other Theatre of Witness projects, after some initial group exercises, we began with the sharing of personal stories. I knew that we'd probably only have time to do one per session, and I had no idea who would volunteer to begin that first day. Kathleen very quickly offered to start. But I feared that if she went first, others might find it difficult to follow the intense grief of her story—especially Anne. So I asked Kathleen if she would be willing to wait for another day. Anne then volunteered. She later said that she hadn't slept the whole night before, as she had been petrified to share her story with the group—especially Kathleen.

Her sharing that day once again opened floodgates of emotion in her, and the group's response was deeply empathic. My faith and confidence in the process with this particular group of women grew exponentially and I knew then that, together, we could make something powerful happen.

When Anne told her story to us, it was easy to see how there was a natural progression of circumstances that had led to her involvement with the Provos (Provisional IRA). She'd been inculcated with republican beliefs since childhood from her family and community, and had lived through some of the most direct violence. For a young girl growing up as she had, joining the cause seemed as if it had been almost inevitable.

> My mammy's brother was shot to death on Bloody Sunday...
> And then after that, everything was about the Troubles. Everything.
> Life was getting stopped and searched, news bulletins,
> Bloody Sunday marches every year, bombs, shootings,
> seeing the Provos' shows of strength.
> Our house was raided a lot in the early mornings.
> One time Daddy was taken off and arrested.
> And one time mother was arrested...
> At age nine at school we made Easter cards,
> and mine had a picture of Mum and Dad, a dead body, and guns.

> When I was 12, I went out with an 18-year-old.
> It was wrong, but it didn't feel wrong enough...
> He showed me a gun when I was 13 and it was exciting.
> I thought Oh my God—I want to be a part of this!
> I want to save Ireland!
> I wanted to save everybody.
> It was a dream. It was an ideal...
> I fancied all the boys who were running around
> in balaclavas and throwing petrol bombs.
> The IRA were our saviors, our heroes, our protectors.
> In my eyes, they could do no wrong.
> At age 13, the Hunger Strikes sealed my fate.
> I became so republican and fired up that I could have told you the names and times of death of each of the hunger strikers.

Anne spoke with great dynamism and excitement. Listening to her, it was easy to imagine her as a young girl being thrilled with the energy of the violent struggle. Her story was vast in scale, yet filled with detailed memories and rich emotional content. When we eventually began to work on the physicalization of her text, I found that she had an ease and comfort with movement as well, all of which contributed to her innate charisma and stage presence.

> Most people who want to become combatants go looking to be.
> But I was asked.
> I was 18 and a fellow I knew well stopped me one day and said
> something to the effect about joining the IRA, and I said,
> "I don't know how you could join the IRA.
> I wouldn't even know who to ask. Why you asking me?"
> And he says, "I'm not asking you to help *me* join.
> I'm asking *you* to join up."
> And, to tell you the truth, I got such a rush that he felt that I was
> good enough and had something to offer more than going on
> marches and demonstrations that I said
> "I don't need to think about it.
> I know what I want to do."
> I'd always felt that, because I was a girl, nobody would want me.
> So that day when that fellow asked me to join up
> I was on Cloud Nine.
> "Somebody wants me for something now, and what better cause
> to be in, than the one that's making us free?"
> It wasn't long after joining that I was assigned to be a quartermaster
> in charge of moving guns and explosives.
> It was a bit like being in sales, and I've been a sales person
> and I was good at it...
> It's hard to be a woman combatant.
> You have to prove that you're up there with them.
>
> You have to never say "no" and always do what you're
> supposed to do, and not let yourself or them down.
> Even though I was terrified and unconfident, when they said
> "This is what we want you to do," I always said "No problem."
> And I might have stood in front of them and said "No problem,"
> but would have walked out the door and thought, "How the F
> am I going to do this?"
> You end up overdoing it and they think you're brilliant.

At one stage I was a unit leader.
There were four men under me and I was their boss.
And I wondered, "How in the world did this happen to me?
How am I going to get four men to do what I'm telling them to
do?" And I never ever knew if I got that position because I was
good enough or because of my boss.
He came on so strong and pressured me sexually a few times,
and in that situation there is no one to turn to. Nobody to talk to.
He was the big boss.
The affair wasn't something that I wanted but I was a soldier.
I didn't know how to say no to people.
People with power and authority used to have me like "that."

Anne spoke about the day she was called to man an explosive
device meant for members of the British Army. She and her partner
waited by the road for their vehicle to pass, but before the army
appeared, she suffered a horrendous headache that later turned out
to be a brain hemorrhage.

I ended up needing full brain surgery.
My daddy held my hand all night long
watching me throw up blood not knowing if I'd live or die.
The life I was leading could have left me close to death by bombs,
bullets, or life imprisonment, and how hard would it have been
for my daddy to hold my hand then?
I believe God works in mysterious ways.
That was one hell of a mysterious way to get me out
of that situation.
It turns out that the Brits were never
gonna come that night anyway,
thank God, because an informer had informed on the whole thing.

But what would have happened that night, was that if we had been
around any longer, they would have picked us up and that
would have been the end of us.
We would have been doing time or maybe even be dead.
But the Brits weren't ever going to come that night. And I'm glad.
Because that's not what I was supposed to be doing.
It's not even what I wanted to be doing.
I wanted to be part of "the cause,"
I wanted to be part of the justice of setting Ireland free.

I wanted to be part of the dream,
but it was never in me to go so far down that road.
It was never in me to be that type of person.
Is it really in any of us?
I believe God said "Anne, you won't stop yourself, I'll stop you."
I would have come so close to pressing the button and
blowing soldiers into smithereens and lived the rest of my life
thinking of their mothers, daughters.
I never would have lived with myself.

Onstage, Anne lay on the top stair, one hand holding her head, the other outstretched. She then sat up and slowly pushed the imaginary button with her thumb. For me, that very small gesture was one of the most poignant moments of the production. Had it happened in reality, it would have destroyed many people's lives, yet in actuality it was such a tiny moment.

Anne's story continued with her leaving the IRA, joining the drug scene for a while, then marrying a man, moving to Limerick, and dealing with abuse from her husband.

I had always had it in my head that if a man hit me
I would hit back no matter what.
The first time he hit me, I hit him back.
And the next time I hit him he fell to the floor.
And I kicked him anyway, I thought I could handle it.
I suppose I thought: "I used to be in the IRA,
I don't have to take this, I'll just hit him back."
I became what I didn't want to be.
A lot of the men who were my heroes
ended up being violent with women.
Maybe some of it was caused by the frustration of not being able
to talk about the Troubles, maybe it was about fighting for power.
It's the damage of war and culture
that doesn't get talked about here.
It took me a long time to realize that the people I'd held up high
as the heroes weren't the heroes I thought they were.
Over the years the disillusionment has grown and grown
and grown. I now think we did it all wrong.
But then, I didn't know any better, didn't see the bigger picture,
and I didn't look to the future to see what could possibly happen.

When I look back at it all now, because I was quartermaster and moving things around the country, I probably was directly involved in getting people killed.

That's real hard to take. I want to learn to forgive myself.

The biggest job I have now is to be the best mother I can be to Asa.

I want to ensure that he'll grow up and be the man
he was supposed to be.

We've been gardening at our allotment together, eating the potatoes and veggies he grew. He's learning the fiddle.

I've done some courses in photography and I am channelling
my energy into creativity.

I'm finally learning to follow my own dreams.

Everybody is ordinary.

We just end up in extraordinary circumstances.

Who the hell can take a journey like this anyway?

Dance Like Nobody's Watching

I met Maria at Robin's house the day we were filming his part for *We Carried Your Secrets*. He'd been nervous about delivering his lines on film, and his partner Maria was the comfort he most needed. We placed her behind the camera, and he got a full view of her caring and radiant face every time he spoke. She displayed passion and intelligence and I knew then that if she was willing, and if it made sense to have a police officer in the second year's show, she'd be a valuable asset to the project. We met for interviews a few times and it became clear that even though her story about being a woman police officer was important, there was other, even more fertile material to focus on, and the concern I'd had not to repeat themes from the previous year's show dissolved.

But Maria presented a huge challenge for me. Once again, because of death threats by dissident groups on police, it was unsafe for her to perform with us. How could I make a radiant and energetic woman appear onstage without actually having her perform live? I knew we could put her part on film, but I wasn't sure that film could do her justice or show her interconnection with the rest of the performers. Her story was so powerful, though, and the filming of it so unusual, that when it was performed it felt as though she was onstage with the rest of the women.

Like so many of the women in our cast, Maria shed many tears during our early interviews and group rehearsals. There is no way to untangle the delicate stories of abuse and abandonment without them. And as in all Theatre of Witness productions, when someone in a cast shares his or her story of abuse, it paves the way for other performers to share their own often hidden experiences of the same. The support among the cast members becomes a vital part of the healing process. After witnessing the beauty of this support among the women in this cast, I was determined to find a way to portray it onstage. Our film-maker John McIlduff came up with the idea of filming Maria full-bodied, straight to camera, with the projection screen being placed mid-stage so as to size her image to be the same as the other performers. The other women sat on stairs surrounding her filmed projection. Slowly and silently throughout her part, they manipulated white strings, unraveling, moving, and shaping them into images that accentuated her story.

I was three when my daddy left our family during Christmas.
My mammy brought my sister and me up all by herself and she made sure our home was filled with music and fun.
I sang in the church choir
and we held wee concerts in our living room.

I danced like nobody was watching.

I missed my daddy.
As the eldest, I thought I had to be the responsible one—
looking after Tracey and mammy.
Maria could always be counted on.
Mammy went back to school and we had to be minded by an aunt—and her house was a place I didn't want to go.
I'd do anything not to go there and be subjected to the things her son would do to me.

But I didn't know how to tell anyone,
so I did it in my own wee way.
I left clues—just as mammy was about to go out the door,
I'd pour too much cereal at the last minute, I'd lose my shoes,

I'd pretend to be sick—even holding onto the door-frame crying
"I don't want to go!"
Sometimes when I was alone, I'd go into our living room,
get on my knees and pray to the picture of the Holy Family:
"Please take me away from all of this!"
But no one ever asked what was wrong.
And my daddy wasn't there to protect me.

My world became black and white.
Everything was tangible and ordered.
I became obsessive and pushed people away.
Relationships with those near and dear to me began to disintegrate
right before my eyes.
There was a tight knot in the pit of my stomach
and I knew what that was.

I was grateful that Maria was willing to mine this bleak and
painful territory to expose her wounds—some still raw. As her
story unfolded and the connection between her childhood and
her choice to become a Catholic woman police officer came to
light, I knew we were once again illuminating the blessing being
born from the wound. I believed that the strength, determination,
and perseverance she displayed would be a powerful model for
other women.

I got married at 21, just to leave it all behind.
But like all unprocessed trauma, the pain and behaviors
came with me into the marriage.
I kept the secret for 24 years.

I never planned on telling anyone, but a family member
talked to me about it happening to her.
One day a special look came between us and she said
"It happened to you too, didn't it?"
That look was the unspoken word.
In a short time, I reported it to the police.
The process kicked in and the police began their investigation.

He was prosecuted and got two years but served only one.
Seeing him there at the trial with his back to me in the dock,
he looked like a wee boy.
I was the adult—and I felt ten feet tall.

I never expected that the male police officers would have been so delicate and caring with me throughout the process.
They were wonderful.
When it was all done and dusted, I thought, "You know what—there are lots of women and men going through similar experiences.
I may just have something to offer them..."

Maria described joining the police and sticking with the difficult training. Being a woman in the police presented challenges:

There's a lot to prove in being a woman in the police service.
Women have to work twice as hard in this job.
Sometimes there's a crowd and you're putting them into the opposite direction to where you're going—trying to keep them safe—but all they see is this wee five-foot three-inch blonde girl and they wonder, "Can she really sort this out?"
But your tactical training comes into play and the adrenaline is going and every single sense is switched on.
Who says women can't multi-task?
I've had to work hard to earn respect from my colleagues as well as the public.
One colleague recently said, "Murphy—I'd follow you into a burning building 'cause I know you'd do the same for me."
When I do a long shift or I'm just so tired that I can hardly move, what keeps me going is the thought that the injured party could be me.
That could be my family sitting in the house with their street cordoned off.
It's about listening and pointing people in the right direction.
Sometimes it's just bringing your humanity...

Given the distrust that so many in Northern Ireland have of the police, and especially of Catholics who join the force, I felt it was especially meaningful for the audience to hear the level of care and love that Maria, as a Catholic woman, put into her role as a police officer. It was another way of breaking stereotypes and contributing to a healing of past wounds.

During the time that we worked together, Maria's relationship with her father was very much in process. The sharing of her story and the support of the other women gave her the strength to rekindle their connection and explore the family legacy. I'd like to think that their renewed relationship was one of the most important outcomes of the performance.

> Over all these years I looked like a strong, independent woman,
> but inside I still missed my daddy.
> I wanted to get in touch with him
> but I was still hurting that he'd left.
> It was like I was standing in the middle of the wee bridge in Bruges.
> I could reach out with my fingertips and touch my mammy with
> one hand and my daddy with the other—but any small step I took
> in either direction could be seen as a betrayal or disloyalty.
> So I stayed stuck in the middle.
>
> But miracles do happen! I took one wee step.
> On his birthday this year, I arranged to meet my daddy.
> We began connecting and talking for the first time in years—and
> we're listening to each other.
> Our family has begun to heal. I have to remember
> it's never too late to try.
>
> I know there are so many girls whose daddies can't
> or won't be coming back.
> For some, it's better if they never do.
> I go to those calls—I comfort those women—
> I listen and I understand.
> Sometimes, all you can do is grieve and mourn
> and then pick yourself up and get on with it.
> And then dance like nobody's watching.

Ruth and Biblical Dreams

> Your people are my people, your God my God.
>
> Ruth 1:16

Biblical imagery is sometimes very real to me. In the mid-1990s I was haunted by visualizations of myself in biblical times, replete with diaphanous garments, bearded men, anointing oils, and "a place at the table." The visualizations were so haunting that I eventually used them as a basis for the text in an autobiographical dance I made about faith. Transforming these images into an artistic exploration of a spiritual path felt like an extension of "midrash," the Jewish form of studying biblical narratives for hidden meanings and interpretations.

When I began teaching Theatre of Witness in the United States, I found that many of the autobiographical pieces my students made could actually be viewed as embodied prayer. This new form seemed to be organically emerging and I longed to integrate it into the larger productions I was making. So one day early on in the process of creating *I Once Knew a Girl*, when Ruth said, "I wish my part could be from the story of Ruth in the Bible," I jumped at the chance.

Ruth and I had been struggling with how to set her part. Unlike some of the other women in the cast, Ruth's story was less about experiences and more about her questions and thoughts about identity and belonging. Ruth told how she had grown up in a "Bible loving, evangelical, and Protestant family in Fermanagh, where the word of God and faith was center stage in our lives." Her family had prayed on their knees together daily and they'd been encouraged to keep themselves separate: "to be 'in' the world, but not 'of the world.'" A bright and deeply inquisitive person, she had explored the boundaries of her identity, being a British, Irish, Protestant woman. She'd been the first woman in her family to go off to university in England where she "studied history of ideas and social work principles." But what I really learned about was "racism, feminism, and being Northern Irish in Britain." I thought that using the biblical story of Ruth as a touchstone might be a powerful way to integrate this Ruth's religious upbringing with her deep questioning about her place in the world—questioning that echoed many of the questions I have about my own life.

Ruth wrestled with the impact the war had on her and her people. She'd grown up close to some of the worst of it—including the Enniskillen bomb that had torn her town apart "not only with grief, but also with conflicting responses about how to best honor the dead."[2] But like many in Northern Ireland, because the violence hadn't directly hit her family, she downplayed the

---

2 The Enniskillen bombing occurred on November 8, 1987.

impact it was having on her. She described a time when she was
away at university:

> One night all the grief I'd held in for years came pouring out and
> I wept all the tears I hadn't been able to shed while back home.
> I was carrying all kinds of grief—a sadness of a people feeling
> beleaguered and misunderstood, and the greater pain of the
> Northern Ireland conflict in whole. It belongs to all of us.

Being away from her homeland gave Ruth the perspective to feel
the magnitude of the conflict's impact. Sometimes it's by changing
our lens of perception that we invite our imagination to see new
possibilities for transformation.

> Today I am interested in a new paradigm.
> Escaping slaves in North America spoke about the five directions:
> North, South, East, West, and Free.
> Maybe "Free" is the mysterious fifth province of Ireland.[3]
> The province of the imagination.
> The place where our personal stories mingle with myth and spirit.
> Where we can ask the tough questions about who we truly are
> and where and to whom we belong without igniting fears
> of disloyalty or reprisals.
> A place of possibility.

I'd been inspired by the concept of a fifth direction named "Free"
after reading about it in a book about slavery. I was entranced with
this concept, and in one of our frequent update meetings began to
free associate about it with Eamonn Deane. He immediately related
it to the mysterious fifth province of Ireland. Ideas and images
seemed to be appearing synchronistically and I knew I wanted
a way to incorporate them in the production. I was reminded of
the Rumi poem I'd used in *Beyond the Walls*: "Beyond all ideas of
right and wrong there is a field. I'll meet you there." We were
imagining and naming a consciousness that was larger than the
one where conflict lay. This all felt like powerful medicine. I knew
immediately that if I wanted to incorporate any of these ideas into
the script, Ruth would be the one who would most identify with

---

3 Ireland is made up of four provinces geographically. The fifth province is a
mythological place where questions may be explored.

them. Luckily, she seemed enthused and, when we incorporated them into her part, it seemed to flow from her with ease and authority.

Ruth's first part was now completed, and it was time to dive into the biblical story to see what fruit it would bear. I wanted to know how she identified with her namesake Ruth in the Bible who'd left her people and followed her mother-in-law, Naomi, into a foreign land. I didn't know what would emerge from our explorations of the text in terms of content or form, but I was excited to lead Ruth in guided imagery and creative association.

There were a lot of tears during our sessions together. It always astounds me how rich the biblical imagery is when fully mined, and how deeply it can touch a personal story thousands of years after its writing. I wish that we had had more time together for this part of the process. In many ways, we could have spent months just on this one biblical story. But as with all Theatre of Witness projects, we're working with a timeline, and we had to keep the creative process moving along.

Onstage, Ruth narrated the story of the biblical Ruth and her mother-in-law, Naomi. She told about the famine in the land that resulted in the death of both of their husbands. She spoke about Naomi urging Ruth to return to her own people, telling her that she had nothing to offer her. She described Ruth cleaving to Naomi, weeping:

> Entreat me not to leave you,
> or to return from following after you.
> Wherever you go, I will go; and where you lodge,
> I will lodge; your people shall be my people,
> and your God my God.
> Where you die, I will die, and there will I be buried.[4]

As the story continues, Ruth followed Naomi into a strange land. They eventually reached Bethlehem, where they gleaned the barley from the fields of a wealthy landowner, Boaz. Boaz saw

---

4 Ruth 1:16–17.

how loyally Ruth looked after Naomi and eventually took her as his bride. Then:

> God gave her conception, and she bore a son.
> The son was named Oved, who became the father of Jesse, who begat Harry, the ancestor of Michael, husband of Mary, mother of Jesus.

I was interested to see how Ruth related to her biblical counterpart and how she saw it relating to the conflict in Northern Ireland:

> I read the story of Ruth and wonder in amazement
> at her resolution and strength.
> But I also wonder about what she doesn't tell us—
> What did she yearn for?
> What was it like for her to leave her people
> and follow Naomi into the unknown?
> Did her family feel she had been disloyal?
> Did she ever go back home?
> And if so, was she still welcomed there?
> In what ways am I like Ruth?
> Who and what would I follow into the unknown?
> What sacred bonds do I have with another or with myself that are as strong and committed as those of Ruth and her mother-in-law?
> Like Naomi who journeyed to Moab, and then returned home—
> I too have come back.
> What do I bring to offer to others?...
> When Boaz left gleanings in the field for Ruth and Naomi,
> it was more than charity.
> It was an expectation to offer kindness to strangers.
> What would it be like now if we offered each other the best of ourselves, our land, our prosperity, our ideals?
> What if we each could say out loud and in spirit:
> "Your people are my people
> Your God is my God"?

Ruth repeated these last lines once as she faced Naomi and Ruth (who were being played onstage), and once with great presence and gravity, facing directly to the audience:

> Your people are my people
> Your God is my God.

It was startling and humbling to hear her declare this to the audience—a group of Catholics and Protestants living in Northern Ireland, a land so deeply divided by sectarianism and politics. Could we really claim each other's people as our own? Could we simultaneously be loyal to ourselves, our people, and our larger ideals of peace? When do we lay down the swords of history and pain? How far will we each be willing to stretch in this new paradigm? And what were we learning from an ancient biblical story?

I picture Ruth standing with her arms outreached to the audience, and I still feel so grateful to her for offering this possibility of an olive branch.

Who isn't Me?

At the end of the day, I want the audience, performers, and myself to come away from every performance bigger in spirit and more emotionally connected with others. I want us all to be able to move beyond dualistic thinking—right/wrong, good/bad—and embrace paradox. And I want us to be able to encompass the fullness of all of humanity within ourselves. To that end, I ask myself how the particular stories of pain, courage, strength, and love seen onstage can be seen to be universal. I look for potent images.

At the end of *I Once Knew a Girl*, I had all the women sit with their backs to the audience as they watched a film projected on the large back wall or screen. The film was a series of cinematic portraits of women and girls, of all ages and backgrounds—from babies to old women in nursing homes. We saw them outside, in their homes, working, and in public settings. They all looked directly at the camera, and their faces were accompanied by beautiful music composed by Brian Irvine. Portraits of the six performers concluded the film. Then each performer came downstage, holding a clear bowl of water in her outstretched hands and introduced herself—not her small individual self that we'd already met, but her largest imagined self: an historical figure, someone they identified with, or someone from a far away land who they never met. They introduced the possibility of an embodied humanity:

> I am Kathleen Gillespie
> I am a judge sitting on a truth commission
> I am the first woman to fly across the Atlantic
> I am a woman who was burned at the stake
>
> I am Catherine McCartney
> I am an Olympic champion
> I am Mother Teresa
> I am the woman whose story wasn't believed
>
> I am Therese McCann
> I am a woman living in a refugee camp
> I am St Therese of Lisieux
> I am the woman whose language is silence and tears
>
> I am Ruth Moore
> I am the woman who was raped and beaten in war—
> collateral damage
> I am one of the first women priests
> I am an artist, creative juices flowing
>
> I am Anne Walker
> I am a medical doctor working in Afghanistan, Sudan, Ethiopia
> I am the woman who had to sell her body for money for food
> I am the leader of a nation

For me, the ending of the show distilled the essence of Theatre of Witness. It is about our capacity to "contain multitudes," in the words of Walt Whitman. It is about recognizing ourselves in each other. It's about understanding how each of our own personal stories is part of the larger tapestry of life. How, born into different circumstances, any of us might have become each other.

Your History is My History

As with *We Carried Your Secrets*, there was a hugely positive audience reaction to *I Once Knew a Girl*. I always like to remember that without the audience, there is no testimony. The audience completes the circle and helps us remember why we do this work. The communion between audience and performers is at the very heart of Theatre of Witness and where the deepest healing lies. Here are some of the audience members' reactions during post-performance discussions or written after the show.

> It draws from the deepness of human experience and in that calls strangers, friends, our fellow human beings into our commonalities, and it shows us how that pain can help us grow. Thank you.

> Heart rending! This performance broke through the seal I have built around my heart to lessen the pain of the last 40 years. It is lovely to see that women can be so resilient and powerful.

> Justice needs a female voice too. It is never easy, but it must be spoken if healing is to come. I hope and pray I never forget this feeling of vulnerability/compassion/discomfort. I want to join in the conversation for peace—whatever that looks like in my life.

> Your history is my history, I hope and trust that the loving space and sacred work will become the future for all us on these islands of the Northern Atlantic.

Home

The women performed *I Once Knew a Girl* more than 14 times around the country, after which I flew back "home." Only this time, I truly didn't know where home was. It seemed as though the center of my belonging no longer had a geographic location. Many years ago, while grappling with this same question of place, a friend had said to me, "For you, home is in the center of your work." I'd resisted this knowing for a long time, but now I began to understand. Perhaps the "fire of creativity" was as real, familiar, and comforting a place within me as any outside place could ever be. I just wasn't sure where I'd be living when it would next be ignited again.

I wondered too about the home for Theatre of Witness. I reflected about the difference in the scale of audience response to Theatre of Witness in Northern Ireland, as compared to the United States and Poland. I realized that, unlike countries where the performers' stories mirrored only a subset of the population (prisoners, refugees, those affected by abuse or violence, etc.), in the post-conflict society of Northern Ireland, each performer's story reflected a piece of the collective and ongoing narrative. Everyone living in Northern Ireland has been affected by the years of violence, whether personally, culturally, economically, generationally, educationally, physically, and/or emotionally. The stories are embedded in the land, history, struggles, and dreams of the people. The scale is large, and there is a lot at stake. It made me wonder if Theatre of Witness had found its new home, even while I myself questioned where I was next to live.

Now, as I discern what is next for me, I am living between countries, waiting for that fire of creativity to be ignited once again. I think about Michael talking about "making home wherever I am," and I wonder if I've come any closer to taking his wisdom to heart. I am filled with gratitude for the blessing of having been invited into the lives of so many extraordinary people and I hope, with the writing of these words, to continue to learn from the lessons they've shared. I reflect, too, upon the evolution of Theatre of Witness and I wonder about its next direction. Maybe it's now time to pass this work on to the next generation. And maybe these words are the first step.

CHAPTER 15

Coda

There is no beginning, middle, end.
There never was a beginning, middle or end.

We Carried Your Secrets

I recently facilitated a workshop in Derry for mental health practitioners. As part of it, I asked people to reflect about how they hold their own story as well as those of their clients. I asked them to make five physical shapes or gestures that expressed the containing of the stories, and then, with a partner bearing witness, to move from shape to shape while speaking improvisationally. Because we had an uneven number of participants, I, too, did the exercise. One of the shapes I made had me standing upright, with my head thrown back, facing the ceiling. My mouth was wide open and both of my hands were gripping my mid and upper chest. The words came out, "I am swallowing the stories. Nothing can go down or up. I am still."

I was moved at the power of the shape, and found it represented an embodied truth. The illness that I have been healing in my body these past three-and-a-half years has been in the cells of the lining of my esophagus. This is exactly the metaphorical place where my body would first be touched by swallowed stories. During the exercise my mouth was wide open. It was hard to discern whether it was screaming, open in wonder and awe, or rounded—ready to receive the next morsel of food. Frighteningly, perhaps it was open in rigor mortis. My hands were touching what was coming down the pipe. Or protecting something sacred. Or holding my heart.

The truth of this shape scared me. It was powerful, yet filled with many possible and paradoxical meanings. Have these 25 years of stories that I've swallowed, digested, and helped to give birth to in new form injured me physically? Or does my esophagus harbor a genetically born wound that is slowly being healed by the very stories I've swallowed? Is my mouth silently screaming? Or is it open, ready for more? Maybe that shape I so spontaneously made was embodied knowledge of one of Theatre of Witness's guiding principles: "The blessing is at the center of the wound." Maybe it's another example of "not knowing."

I also made another shape during that exercise, the final one in that series. I was prostrate on the floor, my legs tucked up underneath me. My back and arms were stretched forward, my chest and face resting on the ground. Slowly I turned my hands over so they were open-palms facing upwards. In a position of supplication and surrender, I exhaled. Ahhhhhhhh.

I want this book to have a pithy end. A quote perhaps from one of the performers that would sum up all that I feel is important. But the truth is that maybe the only way I can conclude is in that last posture. Humbled and questioning. Ready to receive. Grateful and not knowing. Listening. Ahhhhhhhhhhhhhhhhh.

Twelve Guiding Principles of Theatre of Witness

1. Not Knowing

Not knowing is at the very foundation of Theatre of Witness. We live in a culture where high value is placed on knowing facts, achieving, proving ourselves, and being right. Not knowing undercuts all of that, allowing us to see things afresh, to come in without an agenda or judgment. It means having a clean slate, being open, and being willing to meet people with little expectation of what the outcome will be.

Not knowing means being willing to work in an area one knows little about, and trusting that the stories will reveal what needs to be known. The performers who have lived the experiences being shared are always the ones who are the experts. Having said that, it's up to the director to choose carefully and wisely when selecting performers and stories. But it means holding everything lightly, trusting the creative process. It also means that there will be times when one truly won't know what to do or say next. It's fine to wait, to listen, to just let oneself be in the "not knowing." Not knowing is a state of open receptivity.

Not knowing is sometimes also about not planning—like in a conversation. It assumes a deep listening that will reveal what is the next step to take, thing to say, etc.

2. Bear Witness

To *bear witness* means to "be with" fully and compassionately. To be willing to be in the suffering with someone and just let it be. It is sometimes the very hardest thing to do. It means not trying to fix, change, or make things different than they are, even if our heart breaks with sorrow. It asks us to open ourselves to the truth and reality of the moment. Some stories are truly unbearable. Stories of horrific abuse, war, and deep, deep pain can bring even the listener to his or her knees. Sometimes all any of us can do is cry with someone. Bearing witness means having an open heart and a strong center, to remain clear and strong. To have a strong back and a soft belly.

Bearing witness is infused in all aspects of Theatre of Witness. It's at the heart of the interview process when the interviewer listens "with the ears of his or her heart." It's embedded in the early group work when each participant tells his or her story as the group listens and then breathes in and out together in unison. It's what the audience does communally when giving their attention to the performers as they share their deepest truths.

Theatre of Witness strives to bear witness both to personal story and to collective narrative. It's important, in creating this work, to honor the individual and particular life circumstances of each performer, while at the same time giving focus to the larger historical, political, religious, social, environmental, and/or spiritual group story that is shared by the cast. Sometimes what is most important is that each performer lends their personal story to the larger narrative that speaks of their people's story or plight. Then the audience is invited to bear witness to the bigger story of a whole people.

3. Find the Medicine

Finding the medicine is perhaps what distinguishes Theatre of Witness from other forms of testimony. It means to find the healing that resides somewhere in a performer's story or persona. In practice, it means to walk with someone through his or her wounds until the place of strength, redemption, or transcendence reveals itself. Without it, stories of suffering might just become a litany of distress, despair, and victimhood. In scripting performers' stories, the question must be asked, "Why does the audience need to hear this story?" The medicine is where the inspiration lies. It's the point at which change occurs—change of heart, attitude, behavior, or belief. It can be a place of forgiveness, fortitude, survival, or even openness and vulnerability. Often it's the place where victimhood changes to survival, and denial into accountability. Finding the medicine can be thought of as a re-imagining of what might originally have been a one-dimensional or "hardened" story in the mind of the storyteller into a story with breadth, depth, paradox, and spaciousness.

In groups, the medicine is often seen in the relationships of the performers—especially relationships across boundaries. To see performers from polarized backgrounds or positions walk in each other's shoes and support each other is often a great inspiration for audiences.

Sometimes finding the medicine is as simple as uncovering a performer's hidden talent and integrating it into their part. It may be discovering that they can find great joy or comfort when certain music or imagery is used. It can be uncovering a moment of revelation, or a show of strength or compassion. Sometimes it comes from going right into the heart of a wound and finding light and beauty there.

4. The Blessing is at the Center of the Wound

It is by going through the darkest wounds that we find the light and blessing. Much as we all often want to skirt around the details and deep remembering of significant pain and/or trauma, I've found that always in the center of the wound lies the pearl of wisdom or the open vulnerability. The blessing is often embedded in what seems unbearable. The fear and constriction one may have around a traumatic event is sometimes worse than remembering the actual wound itself, if done through a safe and supported process.

Sometimes this process reminds me of traveling to the eye of the hurricane. In that quiet place of balance, around which great upheaval and tremendous waves of energy have been unleashed, lies a knowing. If one can accompany someone through the chaos to that place of equilibrium, a jewel is often revealed. It may be a sense of strength, a feeling of purpose or destiny, or a new insight. Whatever it is, it holds great potential for freeing up the grip of the wound. The expression of that awareness is often what audiences will be most inspired by.

In this work, one often has to go to the center of a story in order to transcend it. As one remembers the details, colors, sights, smells, sounds, feelings, and thoughts, right through to the most specific, often new meaning around an event can be found. New imagery may emerge and, through that, a sense of a broader, more universal story that is shared by people globally. It is often within this new understanding of the universality of the wound that the blessing is found.

5. Deeply Listen with the Ears of Your Heart

Deep listening means listening 360 degrees. It means listening with one's ears, eyes, and intuition. It means to listen for the silences between thoughts. Listen for repetitions and blank spaces. Listen for body language and non-verbal cues. Listen to interpersonal connections within the group. Listen to your own reactions and monitor them carefully. Mostly it means listening without the judging mind.

There will be times in this work when participants will reveal terrible acts they've committed, awful thoughts they've had, or, even harder, demonstrate personal qualities that are disappointing. One's own prejudices and fears will get triggered. The director will hear things they wish they hadn't heard, know things they wish they didn't know. Within these unfolding stories, one's task is to just listen with as much of an open mind and heart as one can bear, or participants will feel judged and probably become less open and more self-blaming.

It's also important to separate one's own personal beliefs from the beliefs and world-view of the person who is being heard. In order to make it safe for participants to reveal their deepest truths, it helps if one can hear the stories from their perspective. I believe that curiosity is the antidote to judgment. It helps if one can ask the "how," "when," "where," and "what" questions.

Yet through this act of active listening, one has to be careful not to confuse judgment with discernment. In creating Theatre of Witness, it's important to make all kinds of discernments about who one thinks is ready to do the work, who will work well with others, and whose story has medicine that will be potent for the audience. It's essential to choose participants who will not inflame, blame, or make judgments of other participants. In this work the entire production is based on the lives, stories, and personas of the performers, and it's up to the director to assemble a cast who will work well together, inspire audiences, and help to create a powerful production. This discernment process is quite different from judgment, which will almost always stop the creative and trust-building process of Theatre of Witness.

6. Become the Vessel

To *become the vessel* means to make oneself the most expansive and purest container possible. In other words, become the love one wants to experience and express. Become vast, as Walt Whitman described when he wrote, "I contain multitudes."

To become the vessel means to continually work on oneself, emotionally, spiritually, and physically. To do this work well, one needs to keep oneself clean and uncontaminated by one's own stories, opinions, prejudices, and fears. I believe it helps to engage in therapeutic processes, both group and individual, to read a lot, to become inspired, to spend time in nature, and to know "the sweet territory of silence." The more one can grow one's capacity to hold, stay steady, and keep the largest possible vision of possibility alive, the more love, trust, and connection will flow. This work in many ways is about allowing the state of "being" to become more important than the state of "doing." It's about being equanimous while at the same time retaining the ability to be passionate and moved. To that end, I highly recommend a meditation practice.

The more a director can become a vessel of understanding, compassion, patience, and love, the more the participants will open up and trust themselves in the Theatre of Witness process.

Lastly, to become the vessel means to follow one's own life quest, questions, and curiosity. It's important to stay connected with that which has heart and meaning, and to look at this work as part of one's own journey. In that way, the themes and questions unearthed by participants need to resonate deeply for the director also. Perhaps a participant's experiences will not be similar to the director's particularity of the stories and images, but underneath that particularity, it helps if there is an underlying connection that deeply resonates with the director. It is that underlying connection that will fuel the creative process.

7. Hold the Paradox

Holding the paradox means holding ideas that may seem mutually exclusive. It means going beyond opinion or belief and being able to accept polarized sides simultaneously. It means balancing good/evil, clean/impure, whole/broken, true/false, violent/peaceful. We are not rational beings. The experiences that happen to us have a multiplicity of meanings. To hold the paradox means to hold them all, even if it seems to be an impossible task. It means not expecting consistency in stories. It means letting things be—even in confusion or seeming impossibility.

To hold the paradox means to enlarge one's sphere of understanding in order to contain these opposites. It means holding the story in a vastness that's bigger than "either/or." It's when a multiplicity of meanings can co-exist that a new paradigm can be envisioned.

8. Find the Gold

To *find the gold* is to find the theme, or the imagery that will be the hook or entry to an individual part or group scene. It can be found in the words or phrase of a performer during an interview or rehearsal, that then becomes a refrain or theme in the script. Sometimes the gold is found as a non-verbal symbol, movement, sound, or interaction. This then becomes the seed that flowers into a central idea. One knows when the gold has been found when there's an "aha" moment in the creative process and everything seems to flow more easily afterwards.

Finding the gold is about finding imagery that speaks symbolically. That symbolism can encompass and envelop a story, giving it heightened meaning.

Lastly, finding the gold means allying with the good, the true, and the beautiful. It means allying with all that will inspire and open the best in people. Find the "vein of gold" that even amidst darkness and suffering will shine some light of goodness and hope.

9. Take the Problem and Make it the Solution

Often in creating Theatre of Witness, there will be times when, for a writer or director, there will be a seemingly insurmountable problem. I used to try to bypass the problems, skirting around them, hoping they'd go away. Later I began to see that they were actually an invitation for creative thinking. Often I decide to take what seems to be a problem and, rather than try to "solve it," turn it into a creative instruction. An example of this was in working on *Years* with older performers, one of whom couldn't discern her direction onstage, when I realized I couldn't trust that she'd even face the audience. So whenever she needed to move to another location onstage, I directed another performer to take her hand and guide her to her next position. The simple and caring beauty of that gesture became an integral part of the production and made the piece more meaningful than if she'd never had the problem in the first place. This guiding principle assumes that "the problem" is actually an invitation to find a new, creative way of doing things that will actually end up being a gift.

10. Fall in Love

Falling in love is like the groundwater of Theatre of Witness. It's about experiencing and demonstrating the qualities of open presence, acceptance, unconditional regard, and care for the performers. Falling in love allows performers to sense that they can open to their deepest wounds and dreams and share them in a trusting and safe environment. It also allows the performers to get intimate with their own stories, which is essential in the scripting.

As the scriptwriter/director, the image I often use is that one "swallows and digests the performers' stories" in order to give birth to them in scripted text. It is an extraordinarily intimate act, which can't be done if there's resistance. The antidote is to be in a state of love. To open oneself to each participant and allow natural feelings of love and tender regard to come through, regardless of what acts the person may have done or not done.

Sometimes falling in love is easier to do than at other times. When I find that I'm having a hard time tapping into that state of love, I know that I need to spend more time in quiet reflection and prayers. I need to open myself to deeper states while being gentle with my own limitations. I need to ask for guidance.

11. Trust the Process

To *trust the process* means to have faith that the foundation and steps of creating Theatre of Witness will work. It means that by staying true to the process, following the guiding principles, and gently opening oneself up into a receptive state, answers and directions will be revealed. Creative ideas will emerge, performers will support each other and carry the load, and the audience will respond positively to the genuine and honest storytelling.

To trust the process means to have patience, and to be willing to ride the waves of uncertainty, obstacles, conflict, confusion, and doubt. These will always be an integral part of the creative process. By allowing these difficult times to just be and recognizing them as a normal part of the creative process, one can trust that they are manageable and will eventually resolve. Knowing and reminding oneself of this, the director can hold the group with confidence and true support.

12. Everyone is Me

This last guiding principle is about learning to see oneself not only *in* others, but *as* "the other." It is about seeing oneself as a refugee, a person who has taken a life, a survivor of war, a person struggling with poverty, or a wealthy landowner. It's about seeing oneself as old, young, male, and female; a Jew, Christian, Muslim, Buddhist, atheist, or agnostic. In the end, with this practice, there is no one who can't be you, no one whose life couldn't be yours, given the same set of experiences, genes, and karma.

This is a hard principle to practice, a hard one to get one's heart around. This goal of seeing oneself in every human life isn't easy to attain. Perhaps it can only be an aspiration. But leaning towards this way of viewing the human condition helps to negate the judging, small mind and invites real empathy and love. Maybe another way to say it is that it encourages communion with the other. It dissolves the boundaries between us and invites one's heart into a vast landscape of interwoven connection. If one keeps this guiding principle in mind while creating Theatre of Witness, the possibility of audience members humanizing "the other" and seeing "the other" as self will be greatly enhanced.

Acknowledgments

I have been blessed with a wonderful circle of friends over the years, without whom, my life would be much less full. You are all deeply meaningful to me and I thank you for supporting and inspiring me in ways that are too numerous to count. Just know that as I write each of your names, years of love and connection reverberate within me. Heartfelt thanks to you my dearest friends and your partners: Billee Laskin, Carol Teutsch, Dan Sipe, Ellen Murphey, Hakim Ali, Hilda Campbell, Jeannie Roggio, Joanna Flanders Thomas, Jon Sherman, Kip Leitner, Lauren Ide, M. Kay Harris, Marian Sandmaier, Nadinne Cruz, Nancy Adess, Naomi and Bob Hyman, Patricia Pearce, Phyllis and Dick Taylor, Ray Kaplan, Rhoda Kanevsky, Sara Joffe, Sara Steele, Sharon Friedler, Susan Teegen-Case, Tyrone Werts, and Yukio Tezuka. And in memory of dear friends who have passed away: Bill Beckler, Carol Sipe, and Ulysses Dove.

Special thanks to Susan Teegen-Case for the beautiful Healing Scroll that is reproduced on the cover of this book. It is a sacred gift for which I'm truly grateful.

Much gratitude to the myriad of people who supported TOVA and Theatre of Witness in the United States and Poland through the years. You, as well as those friends named above, have all been part of a web of support that allowed the work to flourish. Thank you for walking with me as, together, we held the container for Theatre of Witness. For anyone whose name I neglected to mention, please accept my heartfelt apologies and know that your time, effort, and care has been of great value: Aisha Richardson, Alan Greenberg, Allen Kuharski, Anabel Armenta, Andrzej Krajewski, Beth Gross, Beth Mingey, Beverly Jackson, Bill DiFabio, Bill DiMascio, Bill Westerman, Bryan Hull, Cathi Tillman, Cathy Gray, Colleen Cox, Custom Video Productions, Cynthia Jetter, Darren Sussman, former SCI-Graterford Superintendent David DiGuglielmo,

Deborah Weinstein, Don Haldeman, Chaplain Douglas Yeboah-Awusi, PA State Representative Dwight Evans, Ed Seiz, Ed Smith, Elizabeth Bennett, Ellen Tichenor, Emily Elfenbein, Ethan Ucker, Ewa Zareba, the late Faye Kahn, Gerry Clark, Gerry Givnish, Gloria Allende, Sister Helen David, Holcomb Behavioral Health Systems, Howard Zehr, Huang Tran, Jacek Luminiski, Jedd Cohen, Jennifer Clement, JoAnne Mottola, John Rich, Joseph Miller, Joy Charlton, the late Judy Lord, Kate LaMonica, Kirsten Turner, Kristyn Komarnicki, Lamont Murray, Lane Taylor, The Lang Center for Civic and Social Responsibility at Swarthmore College, Laura Forde, Leland Kent, Lili-An Elkins, Lorraine Alesi, Lorraine Stutzman Armstutz, Marek Lagodzinski, Margie Dubrow, Margie O'Keefe, Maria Fernandes, Mark Jackson, Mary and Howard Hurtig, former SCI-Chester Superintendent Mary Leftridge Byrd, Michael Meltzer, Mike Hennelly, Miriam Margles, Nancy Fuchs Kreimer, Nancy Johns, Nancy Savoth, Natalia Danielecyk, Painted Bride Art Center, Pamela Superville, Pat Armenia, Patented Photos, Pennsylvania Volunteer Lawyers for the Arts, Peter Solomon, The Philadelphia Cathedral, Project Home, Rabbi Brian Walt, Rachel Gartner, Rebecca Subar, Renee Atkinson, Renu Rajpal, Robb Carter, Robert Sunshine, Rothang Chhangte, Ryan Burg, Sandy Sparrow, Sara Narva, Stephanie Harper, Susan Berryman, Susan Hodge, Susan Lowry, Suzette Salmon, Swarthmore College, Sylvia Briscoe, Ted Corbin, Thom Yarnal, Tomek Jaksik, Tony Wolfe, Tonya McClary, Tovah Rosenberg, Treb Lipton, Tyrone Werts, Victoria Greene, Wendell Potter, and Will Stockton.

Tremendous thanks to my new Northern Ireland friends and supporters of Theatre of Witness, especially: Eamonn Deane and Pauline Ross, without whom none of the work here would have been possible, as well as: Billy Campbell, Bishop Street Friends Meeting, Caitlin O'Neil, Chris McAlinden, David Grant, Denise Crossan, Eamonn Baker, Elaine Forde, Emma Stuart, Fionnuala Deane, Hector Aristizabal, Hjalmar Joffre-Eichorn, Holywell Trust, James King, Jim Skelly, Jo Noble, John Donaghy, Katie VanWinkle, Magdalena Weiglhofer, Maia Brown, Margie Bernard, Mark Phelan, Maureen Hetherington, Max Beer, Niall McCaughan,

Nicky Harley, Nina Quigley, Pat Kenny, all the support staff at The Playhouse, Rob Evans, Roy Arbuckle, Samia Abass, Sara Brajtbord, Tom Saunders, Tony and Carmel Carlin, and Ursula and Niall Birthistle.

Theatre of Witness is a deeply collaborative process, and none of it would have come into fruition without the expertise and care of artists, composers, and film-makers.

For extraordinary music, I thank: Brian Irvine, the late Dan Kleiman, Dominik Strycharski, Greg Scott, Heath Allen, Kitty Brazelton, Natasha Jitomirskaia Hirschorn, Niyonu Spann, and Wojceich Blecharz.

Film-makers who created lasting and potent imagery include: Carleton Jones, Custom Video Productions, Declan Keeney, Gary Gray, John McIlduff, Laurie White, Margo Harkin, Melvin Epps, Michael DiLaurio, Mitchell Owen, Rachel Libert, and Yvonne Leach.

To my seminal dance teachers, who taught me about embodiment, creativity, bravery, and beauty: Bill Dixon, Dan Wagoner, Judith Dunn, Martha Wittman, and Merce Cunningham.

To my spiritual teachers, who both in person and through their teachings have opened the doors to wisdom, compassion, and greater consciousness: Angeles Arrien, David Crump, Jack Kornfield, Lama Surya Das, Pema Chodron, Rabbi David Cooper, Ram Dass, Shoshana Cooper, Thich Nhat Han, Tsultrim Allione, and my dearest dharma sister Billee Laskin, who continually reminds me of the biggest possible picture.

Deep gratitude goes to: John Steidl, and Drs Mohan Gurubhagavatula and Oleh Haluszka for supporting my healing.

Thanks for editorial support from: Daniel Immerwahr, Eamonn and Fionnuala Deane, Marian Sandmaier, and Nancy Adess.

I want to especially thank: my children Daniel and Adam Immerwahr, who have become men I'm proud to know; siblings Michael and Stephen Sepinuck and Phyllis Epstein for sharing my early years; and my cousin Joan Shulman who has carried on the spirit of my grandmother, Tessa Kurtzman Sepinuck. Deep thanks to my late parents Elaine and Sam Sepinuck for providing me with all the opportunities to follow my heart and dreams.

I offer my most heartfelt thanks to all Theatre of Witness performers whose stories and script excerpts contributed to this book. For reasons of confidentiality, I have chosen to change many of your names here. To all of you, as well as to the scores of other Theatre of Witness performers who have so courageously shared your stories, time, wisdom and spirit to create healing, I deeply thank you. Those who are living, those who have passed away, those behind bars, and those who are free. May all of your efforts be a blessing.

CPSIA information can be obtained
at www.ICGtesting.com
Printed in the USA
BVOW11s1001150817
492102BV00015B/68/P